CW01116755

The Lotus Generation

one woman's hilarious story of her life's travels and travails

---

Carole McCall is a former Civil Servant and Business Woman who has worked as a Life Coach, NLP Trainer, Psychotherapist and Hypnotherapist for many years. Working in the United Kingdom, Ireland, Spain and America, she has helped many people to solve their own problems. This book is about her adventures when her children were grown up and she went to live and work in sunny Spain, and her travels to faraway places including Hawaii, Panama, Costa Rica, Canada, United States and Europe. She is a Grandmother with seven small children and lives in Tunbridge Wells with her husband and a little white Bichon Frise called Stella. *The Lotus Generation* is one woman's hilarious story of her life's travels and travails.

By the same Author –

The Fourth Generation

The Lotus Generation

one woman's hilarious story of her life's travels and travails

Carole McCall

Arena Books

Copyright © Carole McCall 2014

The right of Carole McCall to be identified as author of this book has been asserted in accordance with the Copyright, Designs and Patents Act 1988.

First published in 2014 by Arena Books

Arena Books
6 Southgate Green
Bury St. Edmunds
IP33 2BL

www.arenabooks.co.uk

―――――――――――

Distributed in America by Ingram International, One Ingram Blvd., PO Box 3006, La Vergne, TN 37086-1985, USA.

All rights reserved. Except for the quotation of short passages for the purposes of criticism and review, no part of this publication may be reproduced, stored in a retrieval system, or transmitted, in any form or by any means, electronic, mechanical, photocopying, recording or otherwise, without the prior permission of the publisher.

Carole McCall
    The Lotus Generation *one woman's hilarious story of her life's travels and travails*

British Library cataloguing in Publication Data. A catalogue record for this Book is available from the British Library.

ISBN-13   978-1-909421-46-2

BIC classifications:-   BTP, BGB, BGXA.

Printed and bound by Lightning Source UK

Cover design

by Jason Anscomb

Typeset in
Times New Roman

Dedicated

to

my husband who still makes me laugh out loud!

Glossary of leading persons featured in this book and their relationship with the author

Mona - mother

Hester - grandmother

Hannah - great grandmother

Miranda - daughter

Ellie, Ruby and Jessica - granddaughters

Gillian - sister

Claire, Joanna, Holly - nieces

Stella - father's partner

Amy and Jane - aunts

Suzanne and Emma - daughters in law

Grant - husband

Theo and James - sons

Harry - brother

Murray - father

Malcolm - brother-in-law

Felix, Hugo, Oscar - grandsons

Edward, Rufus, Rupert - nephews

Preface

"Living is a magical thing. Each day is a gift to be treasured, because it will never come around again. We have everything we need, within us now, to live the life we want to live. Consider that most amazing of journeys, a life full of possibilities"

This story is about my life and about the choices I made and the heart-searching and hilarity that I experienced on the way. It is about the search for freedom, both emotional and physical. The freedom to make a choice and then to take complete responsibility for whatever we have chosen. It is about the importance of having a real sense of self and ultimately peace of mind about our decisions.

How do we make a choice? Well that's easy, we use our value system. What is a Value System? This represents a person's sense of right or wrong, in fact what they think ought to be. A value system is a consistent set of beliefs and principles. Your personal values provide a reference for what is good, important and beneficial in your life and it is the personal belief system by which you live your life. Your cultural values help you live in society and these are the norms and principles of expected behaviour.

What is a Belief System? Beliefs are the views and generalisations of ourselves and the world that we cannot change by logic, information or reason. The word "because" either stated or implied often indicates a belief. "It is so because I say it is so!"

What is Cognitive Dissonance? The stress that is actually experienced when a person holds a particular belief or value system and then acts in a contradictory manner. Dissonance is the excessive mental stress and discomfort that can be experienced, when the individual holds two or more contradictory beliefs or values.

What is Human Behaviour? A range of actions exhibited by humans that are influenced by values, culture, religion, attitudes, goals, emotions, genetics, authority, persuasion and beliefs.

What is your Spirit or your Soul? This is an intrinsic part of a person that experiences deep feelings and emotions but is not physical and has many different names in many different cultures.

THE LOTUS GENERATION

What is a Goal? Goals need to be specific, measurable, attainable, and most importantly, time bounded, otherwise it is not a goal it's just a pleasant dream.

This is the story of my choices in the next phase of my life with a restless, distracted husband, a demanding father, three powerful adult children and an uncertain future stretching out before me.

From early childhood I had been brought up with a strict set of rules and boundaries both religious and moral. These directives were complex and convoluted but the message was clear. "You must be good"…… Well you could fill any noun you like in here. Duty bound daughter, solicitous mother, faithful wife, industrious employee, dependable sister, friendly neighbour and the list goes on.

The idea of duty is never more profound than in the Girl Guide Motto, which I remember clearly even now. I had recited this at seven years old and it still applies to all areas of my life. "A Brownie thinks of others before herself and must do a good turn every day."

Along with the majority of women in the world, of every faith or none, I had been determined to do my very best every day of my life. I had worked hard both in the home and at the office, stayed married through difficulties and most importantly put my children through their education. I had watched them develop into the adults that they were really meant to become in the world.

Married in my teens I had three children by the time I was 25 years old. Feminism had struck me like a bolt of lightning in the late seventies. The eighties saw me working my way up the professional ladder, making my own bread and yoghurt and following my husband around the country with his career.

The most important thing in my life was my children and I did the very best job I could do to ensure their happiness and success in life. Wherever we lived, every single Sunday was a family day. When they were younger we went to Sunday school and when they were older we walked in the hills and had a delicious picnic.

I strove to be a caring mother, faithful wife, dutiful daughter, good school governor, contentious employee, responsible chair of the PTA and a cordon bleu cook.

The downside was that I was absolutely exhausted most of the time and just a little cranky, like the majority of women who try to fit too much into every day. The upside of all this is that in your heart you know that you are a really good person who is obeying all the rules.

The prize for all this is that you can hold your head up high and survey the world from a lofty height. You are obeying the rules. You are one of the dutiful people and although the air up there is rarefied you deserve the applause and plaudits because you are doing the right thing.

Except did you stop to ask yourself where your rules and values came from? Did you really know that by saying "Yes" to one person you were actually saying "No" to something or someone else? The rules that you obey and the answers you give to different people could be storing up trouble for the future. The light at the end of this particular tunnel really could be a train coming towards you. The really startling news for most rule-obeying women is profound. I am going to say this really loudly, "You matter too, yes you really do!"

Think carefully about your health, wealth, safety, happiness and future and to do this you will need to address your personal value system so that it includes your own wellbeing.

This process is not about your chronological age, it is about the age of your family and those responsibilities. Your family includes your spouse, parents and children but also includes partner, grandchildren, friends and anyone you love dearly or feel you have a responsibility towards.

You will know instinctively when you have reached the next phase of your life when responsibilities are less intense, but you do also have to know who you are, at this time. You also really have to know what you want, before you embark on the next adventure.

Remember....Whenever you say yes to one person you are saying no to somebody else. This rule applies even if that person is just you!

There is also something that you really need to think about. You really will not feel any different inside no matter what age you are. Sometimes you will be startled by the face that looks back at you in the mirror, but the young child and the older woman are the very same being inside their soul.

THE LOTUS GENERATION

It is not the passing decades that change you. It's about how well you feel and how much care you take of yourself both physically and emotionally. So try each morning to put a little moisturiser on your face. Eat healthily, drink lots of water and dance in the kitchen every day whether you are seventeen or seventy plus.

No matter how old you are, you are still entitled to romance, fun, adventure and education in your life.

Even if you feel really unwell or unhappy try to focus on one positive little thing. Recently I spent six weeks in hospital with tonsillitis caught from a small child and every day, even though both arms were attached to drips, I gave myself a mini manicure. The act of putting on hand cream, filing my nails and buffing them to sheen, calmed and focused my mind. I left hospital covered in bruises from all my blood work but had the most beautiful nails.

The biggest gift you can give yourself and everyone around you is to have a positive sense of self. Have a little mantra that you say to yourself every morning after you have brushed your teeth. "You really can do it!" is as good as any. Choose your own saying then look right into the mirror as you say it. Then smile at yourself with your eyes and notice the difference. Remember everything you need is within you right now.

Looking at your value system very clearly before you go onto the next phase of your life means much less heartache all around. Your treasured values and beliefs are bound to have shifted and matured as you go through life. Write them down and move them around until you feel comfortable that they most closely represent the person that you are now...

Change is neither a bad not a good thing it's just part of the human condition. You know so much more than you did five, ten or twenty years ago.

If you are struggling with conflict with a person or a difficult decision you have to make, do three simple things.

1. Put out two chairs facing each other. Sit in chair one and really look at the situation from your own point of view. Feel what you feel; then say what you have to say out loud.

2. When you are ready, go now and sit in the opposite chair. See things from the other's point of view. Picture what it looks like.

THE LOTUS GENERATION

Breathe in slowly and take your time to do this. Whenever you are ready stand up and give yourself a little shake to release your feelings.

3. Then step to the third position. Stand tall and look at the two chairs with an overview of the situation and see the whole thing with much greater clarity. This is called having a perceptual position. From this information you will be in a much better position to make the right decision for you, for now. You will have a choice...

Some of the heartaches I have experienced in my life have been because I still needed to be that good person and it just was not physically possible to be all things to all men, in my search for personal freedom and peace of mind.

My father came to live with me when my mother died and it worked happily for years. Then my husband had a heart attack and triple bypass and my father still insisted on all my attention.... Who did I choose?

My husband was really restless and wanted to see the world but I still felt that I had family commitments even though my children were fully grown and married... What did I do?

My career meant that I was invited to work in many different places. It became clear that my husband really resented this.... How did I deal with this?

These decisions caused me heartache because I could not please everyone. So who matters most your parents, your partner, your children, your grandchildren, your friends or your career?

The unequivocal answer is that once your children are independent then the person who matters most has to be you. If you keep giving away your emotional and physical energy without thinking about it, then eventually there will be nothing left in that particular bank account. Your time and energy is a finite resource which should be valued and used judiciously.

Make decisions that you can live with confidently and happily and accept it if the people you care about are occasionally unhappy with you, as that is just part of being alive.

Do not, whatever you do, be forced into giving quick answers to other people's questions. Remember you cannot say yes or no in a vacuum and you can ask for time to decide. Practice saying out loud,

"I will think about this and if you want a decision now then I am afraid it has to be a definite no."

Let your unconscious mind be your ally. Your conscious mind is the tip of the iceberg; your unconscious mind is the iceberg below the surface and includes memory, thought processes and motivation.

You know more about your unconscious thought processes than you think you do. Notice that feeling in your solar plexus when something happens or you get asked a question. That network of nerves just behind your stomach will very often register how you feel just before your conscious mind kicks in. Taking time to recognise those feelings and then time to mull things over before making a decision can save years of anguish.

I have learned some things in my life which I think are useful in this context.

1 Never, ever worry what people are thinking about you in any situation, because actually they are not thinking about you, they are too busy thinking about the impression they are creating. Everyone cares about the impression they are making.

2. Try hard not to have an opinion on someone else's life choices and appearance. They have brushed their hair this morning, they have looked in the mirror and they think they are fine. The world would be a less colourful and drearier place if we all looked the same.

3 You really can choose how you feel in a morning. On any ordinary and uninteresting old day you can choose to be cheerful and at peace. Stop whatever you are doing and be fully present and mindful in that moment. Breathe, deep down into your chest, release, then reset your personal barometer and spread the positivity with a smile.

4 If you have serious health, money or family problems that threaten to overwhelm you then you really are perfectly entitled to feel what you feel. However you must remember to take care of yourself, no matter how heavy the burden on your shoulders. Go for a walk, buy a bunch of colourful flowers or read a book or magazine. Thus, allowing yourself a little downtime from the worry and stress will recharge your batteries and help you to cope with your problems.

This is the story of a phase of my life that involved change and challenge. Although it has been lots of fun it has also been filled with some difficult heart-searching. I think I definitely lost my perfect person status along the way; however I gained some real self-esteem and definite peace of mind.

PART ONE

CHAPTER 1
Is That The Dawn Chorus?

> A bird does not sing because it has an answer. It sings because it has a song.
>
> *Chinese proverb*

There is a delicious state between sleep and wakefulness where you have nothing except a faint sense of sadness or wellbeing. The tendrils of reality slowly weave their way around your unconscious mind and you begin to notice. Your heightened senses absorb the first sounds and scents around you. In the distance you may hear the birds and the exquisite, sensory sound of the dawn chorus or nearer, the soft whistling snore of the person sleeping next to you. Then the perfume of the expensive face cream on your pillow teases your nose and you notice the state of your physical being.

Is that the sun on your face and does this feel like your own bed? You stretch one leg luxuriously and then the other one and familiarity assails the senses. Your eyes are forced ever so slightly open by some invisible force. Yes, those are your drapes shifting ever so slightly in the breeze.

Then a quick check to make sure your body is in working order before gingerly raising yourself up on one elbow to pick up the glass by the bed. The last of your five senses is assaulted by the warm water that has been out all night on your night stand. "What time is it?" you croak before peering at the clock. You turn on the radio and the sound of Radio Four completes your journey into reality. That is of course unless you have been dragged out of your slumber by a small child bouncing on you, a cute little dog nudging your face or the clamorous noise of a very loud alarm clock.

The morning in question I had been startled out of my reverie by a small white dog called Stella. Partly Bichon Frise but mostly

THE LOTUS GENERATION

Maltese Terrier she ruled my days. A bundle of white fur with two brown eyes peeping out, she was ready for her morning walk around the garden. I realised that I was sitting in my favourite armchair and feeling decidedly chilly.

I peered at my watch and realised it was only five a.m. As my senses returned the first thing I noticed was that the room was filled with flowers. Not just any flowers but particularly stately lilies, burgundy roses, lily of the valley and gypsophillia and all the arrangements looked identical. There were at least a dozen of them on the table, the piano and the window ledge and the scent was delicious.

Lilies are majestic, burgundy roses for unconscious beauty, lily of the valley for return of happiness and gypsophillia means everlasting love.

As I tried to get up I realised that I must have been sitting there for some time. My neck was stiff and my back was locked. I also assumed by my pounding head that I had partaken in more than one glass of wine the evening before.

I slowly crept into the kitchen and the aroma of Blue Mountain Arabica coffee reached my nose first. Standing at the sink smiling, was my husband with a tiny gold box in his hand. "Happy 30th wedding anniversary, darling" he said rather too loudly for my head. He took me in his arms and whizzed me round at breakneck speed. "Hurrah," Grant shouted "the whole thing was just perfect".

Then I remembered that yesterday we had danced at our daughter's wedding…..

We had enjoyed the sounds of the most wonderful jazz band. My dear friend Cathy was married to a gifted musician who had played the trumpet with Humphrey Littleton for thirty years. Pete had a new band with some of his jazz friends and Coral, the delightful singer had a deep smoky voice. My favourite song of the evening was her perfect rendition of Fats Domino's *Blueberry Hill*.

CHAPTER 2
The Lovely Morning

Not the day only, but all things have their morning.
French proverb

As we strolled, quietly around our lovely garden I could feel the cold, wet dew seeping through my summer sandals. The early morning autumn light was golden and soft. This was my favourite time of year in every respect. As Grant opened the greenhouse door I saw the last of the tomatoes, inter-planted with perfumed basil, deep red and heavy with the summer sun that had seemed to last forever.

Then on the breeze that delicious ripe aroma of the purest of nature's culinary combinations teased my olfactory senses before it drifted away slowly like plumes of smoke into the ether.

The autumn chrysanthemums stood like formal Swiss Guards to attention in every shade of bronze, purple and pink. The sparkling white cosmos looked as bright as the summer morning when I had planted them. As we walked along I realised that it was the trees that were the stars of the show.

We had a row of silver birch trees whose bark cast a ghostly light in the evening but they looked a pearlescent white in the early morning sun. I love Acers in the autumn and the vivid shades of green, red and yellow leaves were all around us. I stood and breathed in the muted colours of the hazy horizon and that autumn scent of ripe quinces and bonfires.

I absentmindedly recognised a faint droning noise as the furry autumn wasps, buzzing in and out of the grapevine. I pulled my cashmere cardigan more tightly around my shoulders and smiled at my husband. Miranda was our second child to be married and we realised how lucky we were in our children's choice of partners.

As we walked we talked excitedly about the wedding. Our daughter and her husband Alistair had set off for the Maldives after their wedding breakfast. They planned to stay for a month and we laughed as we reminisced about our own honeymoon on the beach in Anglesey. We drove there, had four hours on the beach and drove home again. I think the reason was lost in the mists of time but was something to do with being students and a car breaking down.

We discussed the wonderful and interesting guests that had come from around the world including Europe, Canada, Australia and America. Miranda kept every friend she had ever had and we have a large extended family.

We had invited nearly four hundred people to the wedding yesterday and it had been a magical occasion. As we strolled along holding hands and quietly talking a slight, imperceptible notion forced its way into my sleepy mind. Not only had we welcomed all those guests yesterday, we had also invited fifty of our nearest and dearest for lunch today.

As I raced back towards the kitchen door I yelled to my husband "You will have to come and help me." I had my hands clasped around my pounding head and failed to notice the hanging baskets that were artfully draped around the pergola.

I stumbled blindly into the fuchsias, geraniums, petunias and trailing lobelia which would normally have entranced me as I passed. That morning all I shouted was "Oh Bloody hell!" as my mind was preoccupied by getting the house ready for fifty guests.

CHAPTER 3
The Lovely Little Box

Gold cannot be pure and people cannot be perfect.
Chinese Proverb

I ran upstairs and into my bedroom and was stopped in my tracks by a heart uplifting sight. Facing me was Miranda's wedding gown hanging over my wardrobe door. She had looked so radiant in her shantung silk dress in the palest of cream. The full length skirt swept the floor and I could still faintly hear the swish the long train had made as it followed her down the aisle. The bodice was exquisitely embroidered with tiny flowers and seed pearls. Her four small bridesmaid's outfits matched hers and they carried pink and cream posies. The four older girls wore deep pink dresses and had

THE LOTUS GENERATION

bouquets of cream lilies. Miranda carried Arum lilies in a 1940s style reminiscent of her Grandmother's bouquet.

The memory of the wonderful day was stowed deep in my heart, to be taken out and examined at my leisure. Now I had a lunch to organise. My friend Helen owned a delicatessen in the village and she was bringing most of the food we needed. Hand-raised pies, a glistening ham, and a series of cheeses and salads of every type. She had also made a sherry trifle and her trademark pavlova, dripping with fresh cream and raspberries.

I jumped into the shower to wash away the mousse that had held my chignon in place yesterday. The stream of hot water was wonderful on my skin and I felt my headache slide away. I could have stayed there forever in a cloud of deliciously scented steam but my gaze was drawn to the cold bathroom window with the rivulets of water running down it.

My pleated blue and white pearl and feather fascinator was sitting on the bathroom window ledge. The rivulets of water on the window pane were dangerously close. Anna who had designed my fascinator for me had carefully matched the coloured silk of my delicious pale blue Paule Vasseur mother of the bride outfit. I slipped a towel around me and padded across the bedroom to place it in the matching hatbox it had come in. I stood on my tiptoes and reached up to put it on a high shelf out of harm's way.

Little did I know that not many years later a little girl with blue eyes and blonde curls would be using it to play dress up and would leave it out in the garden, on the swing, in a torrential downpour of rain?

As I dressed in my new crisp linen trousers and silk shirt I thought about my mother, Mona. She had died five years earlier in her early sixties and I missed her every day. Even now I pick up the phone to ring her when something happy or sad happens to me. As I begin to dial her number realisation hits like a hammer blow and I have to take a few minutes to centre myself.

My father Murray had come to live with us about three years after he was widowed. He was only seventy one years old but seemed as though he was much younger, with his energy and enthusiasm. He had always lived in the North of England and found living in the

THE LOTUS GENERATION

Home Counties very different to his earlier life. He had got involved in the community playing bridge and running an allotment but he was always looking around the next corner for something new.

The advent of the BBC Parliamentary Channel cheered him up enormously and he would be found sitting on the old leather armchair in the study, commenting vociferously on the state of the economy. He also enjoyed watching former colleagues from the unions who had become MPs in the previous year's Labour landslide.

It was a pity my mother had not lived to see Labour's victory of the previous May. She thought very highly of Tony Blair personally and would have loved to see him as Labour prime minister.

Our guests started to arrive and we spent a wonderful relaxing day and everyone from the oldest uncle in his nineties to the newest family member joined in the fun.

The sun was still shining and so people were relaxing, on the terrace and in the conservatory, meeting up with old friends. The music that day was a combination of Robbie Williams, The Corrs, The Manic Street Preachers and Leanne Rimes singing "How do I live without you".

We also had Tony Bennett, Frank Sinatra and of course the Beatles for the more discerning. We had invited all the neighbours as well so there thankfully no complaints!

As the evening approached most people had gone to catch their planes, trains or automobiles home. Some of the younger relatives that were staying were lounging about watching episodes of the Simpsons and Men Behaving Badly. I popped my head in the kitchen and saw my two sons James and Theo putting the world to rights with my father Murray and their father Grant. I thought this is my cue to slip away for an early night.

As I climbed the stairs I realised how lucky I was to be living in a world where people who live so far away from each other could still be close. As I went into my bedroom I remembered the tiny gold box Grant had given me.

Nestled inside the box was a perfect circle, a Clogau ring made from Welsh gold. "He is so thoughtful" crossed my mind "He has remembered that Miranda was born in Wales."

THE LOTUS GENERATION

As I was drifting into sleep I thought about my lovely daughter and her perfect husband. I wished them a wonderful honeymoon six thousand miles away on the other side of the world.

I felt rather dejected after the excitement of the lovely wedding was over. I had worked very hard to make it a special occasion. I was still in my forties and my head was spinning with plans, as I wanted to do so many things with my life.

My body was not always able to keep up though because I had been diagnosed with relapsing and remitting Multiple Sclerosis in my twenties. In between the relapsing spells I felt fine and could rush around like a twenty year old. When a relapse happened I stayed home and felt more like an eighty year old. I had had so many MRI scans, head spinning lumbar punctures and other tests but tried to keep all that to myself.

I had lots of experience dealing with other people's problems but I knew that the skills I possessed meant much less in my own life. When facing a difficult issue I shunned the celebrated words of Virginia Satir, Fritz Pearls or Milton Erickson and I opted for the wiser words of an altogether more down to earth counsellor, blue haired Marge, mother of the Simpsons family.

"It does not matter how you feel inside, you know. It is what shows up on the outside that counts. Take all your bad feelings and push them down, all the way down, past your knees until you are almost walking on them. Then you will fit in and you will be invited to parties and boys will like you. Happiness will follow."

Of course my head knew this was not sound advice but it always made my heart smile and that was just the thing!

In my experience when people ask "How are you?" They want a cheery "I am really well thank you," not a litany of your latest health issues. It is not that people do not care; they just have a lot going on in their own lives. Smile and the world will seem brighter already.

I was enjoying my life coaching practice and revelling in using my brain again after some time off work. I loved all things domestic like gardening, making things and cooking but like most women I needed to use my brain as well.

CHAPTER 4
Shall We Go To The Dordorgne Next Year?

Holidays, a period of travel and relaxation where you take half the money and twice the clothes you need.

Anon.

At the start of the last year of the twentieth century the European currency was launched. I felt, a little selfishly, that the euro was good news for travellers like us as we would only need to do one exchange from sterling to euros.

The Labour government announced that they had no plans to join the euro and would be staying with the pound. I really wished my mother had been around to see the minimum wage introduced and a particular favourite of hers Neil Kinnock was made vice-president of the European Commission. She had always admired the past Labour leader and felt it was a pity he lost the 1992 election.

A devastating combination of dancing to D' Reams anthem "Things can only get better" at the party the night before the election and his apparent presumption of victory seemed to alienate the voters.

A newspaper headline stating "If Kinnock wins today will the last person to leave Britain turn out the lights." sealed the deal for the Conservatives and John Major formed the new government.

John Major was known for a few gaffes that made it into the Coleman Balls column of the magazine Private Eye. "When your back's against the wall it's time to turn round and fight".

This satirical magazine was my mother's favourite read and you could not disturb her the day it was delivered. She was so proper although it was ok to laugh if it was in Private Eye.

Her favourite Colman Balls by far was the famed utterance by distinguished cricket commentator Brian Johnson: "The bowler's Holding, the batsman's Willey!"

One of the most expansive plans made in the days after our daughter's wedding was for a holiday in the Dordogne. Twenty-two separate but related people from three different countries were about to spend three weeks in an old large but dilapidated and ramshackle farm house.

THE LOTUS GENERATION

As with all great holiday schemes the excitement is in the planning and many long distance calls were made that spring. Nobody quite remembered who actually knew the friend of a friend who owned the villa. It was with some trepidation that we arrived the day before our guests from Spain and Canada were due.

As we drove passed Hautefort Castle and over the bridge across The River Dordogne we became a little perplexed by the road signs. We were travelling with our daughter Miranda and our daughter-in-law Suzanne. The girls were delighted to have sunny days without a plan stretching before them and sang Abba songs the whole way. *Take a Chance on me* and *Dancing Queen* were their particular favourites. Their husbands Theo and Alistair were due to join us a week later when they finished work.

I asked Grant to stop for directions near a tiny boulangerie and I leapt out of the car before he could argue. The shop smelled wonderful and was full of croissants, pan au chocolat and crispy loaves of French bread standing to attention.

The interior of the shop was gloomy after the bright summer sun. As I adjusted my gaze I saw a young woman looking haughtily back at me. In my haltering French I started to ask her if she knew where the village that we needed was situated. She put her hand up like a policeman in rather an imperious manner.

"Stop, stop, Madame, do I look like the kind of woman who cannot speak English?" I hung my head in shame although I was not quite sure why. "Oh" I said and wished I had not asked for her help. With that she pulled her pinafore over her head and said "The shop is not busy, I will close up for a few minutes. Wait for me at the front of the store."

As I got back into the car, she whizzed around the corner in an old Renault and took us the ten miles that we needed to go. We waved our thanks; she scowled and was on her way. I love it when something unexpectedly good happens; it confirms your faith in human nature!

The farmhouse loomed large into view and we all stared hard as we had not really known what to expect. Grant opened the door with a huge key that, as directed on his notes, was under the third stone on the left. The door creaked as he pushed it open and the four of us peered round the corner. A dim pall was cast over everything and a solitary mouse took a moment to stare at the intruders and then scurried across the stone kitchen floor.

"Great start" mumbled Grant as we stumbled forward. We all fanned out to investigate the rambling house and discovered that there were nine bedrooms on three floors. Enough for all our guests in comfort we calculated. On the third floor there was an attic bedroom with a huge four poster bed with an old iron chandelier perched precariously over it.

I reached out and gently patted my hand on the old damask bedspread. It had that vaguely cold, damp feeling that sends shivers down your spine. "We will take this room" I whispered to my husband as I thought the rest of the house might be warmer for our guests.

Slowly over the next two days they began to arrive. My aunt Amy and her husband John from Vancouver. Their son Joshua was on his first extended trip away from his law office in many years and my father Murray was travelling with him. Our son James and his girlfriend Isobel were coming on the train from Paris.

My sister Gillian and husband Malcolm drove from Spain in their car. Their two children Claire and Rufus came on the coach from London. Our neighbours from the Lakes, Jane and George were holidaying with friends nearby, but were going to spend a few days with us. Our son Theo and son-in-law Alistair would make the full complement.

The bedrooms were organised to everyone's satisfaction and we talked about how we were going to divide kitchen duties. Lawyer Joshua had a bright idea. "Why don't we put everyone's name into a hat and pull out two names at a time. Those two people will shop, make breakfast, cook supper and tidy up the kitchen. That way everyone only has to work one day of the holiday and people will get to know each other really well.

I could not believe we had not thought of this before. We had lots of holidays with groups of family and friends and there was always one person who did too much and one person who got away without doing a thing.

THE LOTUS GENERATION

Over several bottles of Bordeaux and a bottle of Armagnac, which was opened late into the evening a plan began to form. There was much laughter as the most unlikely pairings for kitchen duties appeared out of the hat. When two people who were known to be great cooks appeared there was cheering. When two hopeless cases appeared there was much laughter and jeering.

CHAPTER 5
We Have Some Wonderful Things To Eat

After dinner sit a while, after supper walk a mile.
English proverb

The first couple to cater for the eclectic crowd were Joshua, the lawyer and Gillian, the headmistress. They were cousins in their forties brought up on opposite sides of the Atlantic. As I walked gingerly down the steep staircase I could hear the two of them laughing. They had just arrived back from the village with arms full of croissants and pain au chocolat for breakfast.

As I looked out through the small, dusty window pane I could see my father sitting out by the pool reading a big, heavy tomb. I wished my sister and cousin "Bonjour" and then went out to ask my father if he would like some breakfast.

As I stepped through the doorway the scent of honeysuckle nearly knocked me over. I looked up and could see that the house was covered with pale green leaves and cream and yellow small flowers. A pale pink rose scrambled through the honeysuckle but I could not decide what variety it was.

As I walked across the garden I heard a cheery hello from the pool. It was my Aunt Amy and she was swimming up and down with a determined stroke. The most accomplished of women, she was as busy in her sixties as she had been in her twenties. She had enjoyed singing all over the world with her Sweet Adeline's choir and could speak perfect French. She also had the kind of laugh that started as a chuckle from somewhere deep inside her. Then the chuckle burst into a musical symphony and you just could not avoid joining in with her.

The real thing that endeared her to me, though, was that she looked just like a younger version of my late mother Mona.

Whilst Murray and Amy were heading in for breakfast I decided to have a look round the garden. I pushed open the rickety wooden gate and to my surprise golden fields filled the horizon. We were in a small dip and the rolling hills around us were filled with majestic and vivid yellow sunflowers. In the early morning they were facing east and I knew that they would track the sun throughout the day to face west. In the dark night they reoriented themselves to face east for the morning sun.

I heard a chugging noise behind me and an old tractor appeared into view and I turned around to stare. To the west of us were shimmering grape vines as far as the eye could see. Then the sonorous sound of the ancient church bell began to chime un , deux, trois, quatre, cinq, six, sept, huit I realised that it was eight am and I was ready for my breakfast.

After a leisurely repast about half the crowd decided to go to Perigueux to do some shopping. Grant and I had been there many times before but wanted to look around the market. The daily market is an important part of life in France and it is fun to have a coffee and a brandy and watch the world go by.

The Dordogne has many famous food stuffs but none more so than the geese and duck products. As you drive through the rolling French countryside you know that you are in the right place by the flocks of white, waddling geese on every farmstead. I remember as a child being told never to go near a goose as its bite is definitely worse than its hiss or honk.

That sunny day we bought half a kilo of walnuts, a large piece of Rocamadour cheese and some of the fat red cherries that were nestling in wooden boxes on the counter.

We noticed our designated cooks for the day, wandering around chatting, picking up this and that and having a wonderful time in the sunshine. I was really looking forward to my evening meal.

We stopped to buy a large Gateau Noix to have with coffee in the afternoon. I asked the lady in the patisserie if she would tell me how the cake was made. Finally after much consideration and flapping of hands, she wrote it down for me. I still have it in the back of my mother's recipe book.

CHAPTER 6
Should We Have A Snooze?

Sleeping is no mean art: for its sake one must stay awake all day.
Frederick Nietzsche

We passed the afternoon reading and snoozing and I could definitely hear a rousing game of boules going on in the far distance. Finally it was time for supper and we all filed expectantly into the dining room after we heard the loud gong.

A huge antique mirror decorated the far wall and then reflected the candelabra and the fragrant lilac sweet peas sitting in a white jug. The table was enormous and matched the stunning armoire that dominated the room.

Supper was a delight for all the senses. Hors d'oeuvres including cold cuts, devilled eggs and paté decorated the table. There was a velvety leek and potato soup to follow. The star of the show was a huge Cassoulet filled with duck, goose and pork sausage in a delicious sauce and made in a deep, round earthenware pot. There was a salad and lots of crisp French bread bought fresh that evening as is the French tradition. Flagons of the local Bordeaux wine were enjoyed by all.

We all moved onto the terrace to congratulate our hosts for the day that had made such a fine start to our elegant plan. Petit fours and coffee were passed around and we enjoyed a game of lively scrabble until bed time.

The next morning I woke early and watched the swallows swooping at the eaves of the house just above my head. I looked out of the window to see my children laughing as they whizzed up and down the swimming pool. They are all excellent and able swimmers, it seemed the years of taking them to swimming lessons had really paid off.

A thought occurred to me. It seems a mother is only truly content in her heart when all her children are safe and well under her roof and the sound of them laughing and enjoying each other's company rings through the air. It does not happen very often but when it does a sublime feeling pierces your heart.

The holiday went on at a lovely pace. New friendships were formed between people who were related by blood, but really had not known each other at all. Close bonds were reinforced and tales of the past were explained in detail and memories regained.

There were different trips out every day but nobody complained if you wanted to stay home and read. The two by two catering plan meant that we ate like kings every day.

We had Duck Confit at least three times as it was so delicious. The wild mushrooms were in season and made delicious soup. The non-vegetarians amongst us had the local dish of Foie Gras made from goose liver and one day we had the most delicious omelette made with local truffles. Walnuts figure all over the region and taste differently when they are green. They seemed to figure in most puddings and the walnut oil and walnut liqueur are good too.

The holiday was over too soon and the Canadian party left early as they wanted to visit the Courcelette Canadian Memorial. John was very keen on military history and this seemed an ideal opportunity to be able to fully absorb the historical context. This memorial is set in a little park where visitors can rest and reflect and I know they felt empowered by their visit.

Some of the others went to Bordeaux to see The Tour de France; the whole area came to a standstill as this is France's greatest sporting event. They told us that the fans all wore the same colour as their chosen team. They thought it had been worth the long wait in the mid-day sun to see the cyclists flash by in a kaleidoscope of colour. They said they had a lovely day and we were glad that they had brought lots of delicious wine back for us.

When the holiday was finally over it took us all a while to pack up the cars. Nobody was desperate to go home and we all agreed the only downside had been the very large mosquitos that had bitten us all. Everybody wanted to take their particular treasures including cheeses of every description. I was actually very glad I was not travelling in those cheese cars.

My absolute French treat is to search out and rummage around the Brocantes whilst I am on holiday. There is a particular assault to the senses in these places that you do not get in English antique or second hand furniture shop.

The French Brocantes are always dark and chilly places with a little old lady in a washed out apron sitting on an old stool near the door. No matter how sunny or warm it is outside the atmosphere always chills you to the bone. The lady on the stool will nod and you will smile and she will leave you alone to examine her treasures. I had spent many hours searching and this visit I had picked up a broken antique dining chair and an ormolu bronze mantle clock.

I was so pleased with my purchases and knew exactly what I was going to do with them when I got home. When the car was full Grant announced that that there was no room for my treasures. I travelled the next ten hours feeling very huffy indeed with a broken chair at my feet and a heavy ormolu clock squashing my knees.

CHAPTER 7
I Am Definitely off Patterns

A girl should be two things: classy and fabulous.
Coco Chanel

Later on that year Grant and I decided to take a last minute break. One of those holidays where you pay your money and a big surprise awaits you. We disembarked at Palma Airport in Majorca and headed for the coach. Grant's face was set into a decidedly serious manner. He hated not knowing where he was going whereas I love an adventure.

Forty minutes later as darkness surrounded us we realised that we were the last people on the coach. Grant opened his mouth to say something snippy as the bus stopped with a judder and we both jolted forwards. It had been a very long journey. As we staggered down the steps we both beamed at the same time as we could see a swish five star hotel in front of us.

The room was elegant and spacious. The walls were painted blue and as I moved the drapes aside I realised we were overlooking the harbour. The lights twinkled and I could hear the rhythmic waves pounding below. Grant asked for supper to be served to us in our room. The waiter brought us Sobrassada which turned out to be a type of delicious pate. We ate this with relish. There was also bread, olives and red wine to be enjoyed.

The next morning I felt as though I was floating on a boat, as the azure room with its billowing white drapes slowly entered my consciousness. "Wonderful" I thought "we have a week doing nothing"

We lounged about enjoying the view and drinking cortado, the Spanish espresso coffee with a dash of hot milk that we both enjoy.I took some time to decide what to wear. Finally I settled on a red and white patterned silk dress that made me feel elegant and slender. Sunglasses and a white straw hat and I were ready to go.

We found a restaurant at the harbour and a waiter showed us to a table. We decided on paella and a bottle of Rioja. I took a sip of wine as I leaned back in my chair to look around. There were around fifteen tables each occupied with a couple talking occasionally in a desultory manner. I noticed with a start, that a variation on the same outfit adorned every single slender woman. Jeans, boots, leather jacket, diamonds and huge sunglasses perched on every perfect retroussé nose.

I looked down at my lovely patterned silk dress and acknowledged that it had suddenly morphed into an alien and unbecoming sack. I felt like the woman who had all the right clothes but was just was not wearing them.

At that moment the waiter arrived with a huge platter of steaming Paella. It looked delicious with its golden saffron rice, prawns and vegetables of green and yellow. As I said "Gracias" to the handsome young waiter I picked my fork and prepared to tuck in. "Heaven" I thought to myself.

Then I caught the gaze of the woman sitting near me. She smiled imperiously and stared at my paella with what I can only describe as distain. I noticed she was putting red wine vinegar and pepper on a plate of tomatoes. I looked around and realised every woman in the restaurant was eating the ubiquitous tomato salad.

THE LOTUS GENERATION

At that moment my delicious lunch turned to dust. Every mouthful was an ordeal and I toyed with my food and refused desert. I saw a little frown appear on Grant's brow and he raised his eyebrows at me.

How could I possibly tell him just what had happened to me? Was I the woman in the lovely dress enjoying a delicious lunch? Or was I the foolish creature who did not know the dress code and had committed a terrible lunchtime faux pas?

As we walked back up the hill I was very self-absorbed. "Listen," I thought "Nobody has said anything to you; in fact you have made yourself feel so bad".

I knew how to change my negative thoughts. "Stop, Breathe, Move.

Your behaviour is affected by your state. Your state is affected by your physiology. Your physiology is affected by your breathing. Breathe in through your nose for the count of four. Breathe through your mouth slowly. It is hard to feel down when you are looking up. It's impossible to feel up when you are looking down."

By the time we climbed to the top of the hill I was ready for an ice cream, but I gave patterns a miss for the rest of the holiday.

CHAPTER 8
The Orange Blossom Express

A man is not an orange: you can't eat the fruit and throw the peel away.
Arthur Miller

We had a lovely lazy week but one day decided to venture into Palma, the capital city of Majorca. Grant loves trains and wanted to go on the Orange Blossom Express. The train to the port of Soller had its own station. There were queues of tourists waiting by the ticket office and we heard people saying "The fare is a Euro".

Grant grabbed hold of my hand and pulled me away from the crowds. He headed for the first class ticket office and said haltingly "Cuanto es un billete de primera?" The assistant laughed and said "It's actually two euros"

THE LOTUS GENERATION

As the train pulled in we noticed the first class carriage was at the back of the train and had its own private balcony. To our utter amazement we were alone in there as the train set off on its journey. To be in that carriage that day was like stepping back in time. Leather seats, panelled walls and brass lights with the polished sheen of a hundred different hands. I felt as though I was in an Agatha Christie novel.

We leaned back to appreciate the splendour and very soon we were in the bright green, deep orange groves. We stood on the balcony and as you gently reached out you could touch the leaves. The scent was intoxicating, white orange blossom and ripe orange fruit made a heady mix.

Valencia orange trees are well known for having fruit and flowers at the same time. This is because the fruit requires around 15 months after blooming before harvest. The new flowers are blooming at the same time as the old fruit is ripening. The smell of the heavy ripe fruit and the heady orange blossom is exquisite.

That journey went so slowly, every minute seemed like an hour to be enjoyed to the full by the five senses. The view was spectacular, fiery orange and green trees with the encircling blue hills in the distance. We heard the sound of the engine and the occasional "toot, toot" mixed with the clamour of excited voices.

The scent and the taste of the sweet oranges and the feel of the leaves brushing your fingers as the world rushed past were wonderful. Too soon we were in Soller and had to change for a tram to take us to Soller Port.

We spent a few happy hours having lunch and sightseeing. All too soon we were waiting for the train to take us back to Palma. We were talking to some young people and told them about our amazing first class journey. As we boarded the old train we were surrounded by students. They had decided the extra euro was worthwhile. We squashed along the seats to give them more room. There were about a dozen of them and one had a guitar and another one a harmonica.

We spent the return journey singing along to their accompaniment. The Beatles, Eagles and Neil Diamond sounded amazing and were fun to join in with... The best part for me however

THE LOTUS GENERATION

were the guitar solos *El Colibri Danse, Du Corregidor*, and *Fandango* which had us all clapping with delight.

As I was drifting off to sleep that night I decided speaking to strangers on a train was definitely a good thing. I also agreed with my husband that a couple of brandies before bed were the perfect end to a perfect day.

The next day we drove to have a delicious lunch in the hills. The restaurant we chose had been run by the same family for decades. The stand out dish was suckling pig which we duly ordered. As the sunshine streamed through the windows I could see tiles sparkling on the walls, floors and ceilings. The suckling pig arrived and as I looked at it I thought "Ooh! I cannot eat that." Grant was happy to eat the pork and I ate the salad.

I closed my eyes in the soporific sunshine and as I was just beginning to nod off the sound of Ricky Martin's *Livin'LaVida Loca* resounded round the restaurant. There is absolutely something about that song that lifts the spirits and it definitely put a spring in the waiter's steps. It was certainly responsible for the summer Latino craze that swept Europe that summer and was heard throughout the Balearics when we were there.

I had done my research and I knew that I really wanted to go to The Born. This area is famous for its flower sellers of every type. I loved the colours that were so vibrant. Every shade of rose, lily, peony and hibiscus showed its face to the afternoon sun. I stood admiring the street scene but I also knew that just across from there was a jeweller famous for its Majorcan pearls.

I fixed my sunglasses firmly on my head and the doorbell resounded like a shot around the shop as we entered the door. There was nothing to see as the sunlight had affected our eyes. Slowly as the stygian gloom began to fade we saw a very large shop full of the most wonderful things. I spent two hours wandering up and down soaking in the beautiful jewellery. There were diamonds, emeralds, sapphires and rubies but best of all to my eye pearls in every hue. I finally chose a double row of smooth, cream pearls and I treasure them to this day.

At the close of the year, to the background of the resurrected song *1999* by Prince they were lots of different concerns doing the rounds. The Millennium Computer Bug promised all sorts of catastrophes. Called the Y2K, the premise was that computers would crash as they would be unable to recognise the year 2000. We all held our breath as the bells chimed but thankfully nothing happened!

Grant and I went into London with his sister Faith and her teenage son, Mark. He was really keen to see the firework festivities and soak up the atmosphere. The reality was very different however as the crowds were enormous and he was quite frightened. Grant, who had not wanted to go in the first place, was a star. He turned us around and somehow got us back to the station and on to the homeward bound train.

We jumped in the car to get back home for midnight but had to stop at the garage because we were driving on fumes. Midnight 1999 found us at the petrol station toasting each other and the bemused shop keeper a "Happy Millennium" with cans of Fanta orange soda.

Here we go again I thought as we catapulted into a new century.

CHAPTER 9
What Are You Doing Out So Late?

The best conversations usually happen late at night.
Anon.

Even though we had not seen the new century start in London we made up for it with a visit a week later. We started with a trip on the London Eye which had proved very successful. We were looking forward to the opening of the Tate Modern the following May. We spent at least one Sunday a month at a gallery or exhibition.

The Queen Mother celebrated her 100th birthday this year and still seemed to be a favourite as she waved to the crowds.

There were two elections that year of note. In the UK Ken Livingstone was elected Mayor of London. We had met him when we lived in the Lake District and liked him and thought he would do a good job for London. The thing that amazed me was that even though there was much to talk about journalists he seemed fixated on his newts.

THE LOTUS GENERATION

Later on that year George W. Bush was elected the forty-third President of the United States of America. We stayed up all night watching the election as it could have gone either way. Al Gore was odds on favourite but after much discussion of "Hanging chads" in the State of Miami George W. Bush was the eventual victor. His close relationship with Tony Blair fashioned much of the next decade.

Our oldest son Theo was thirty years old that year and we all went to a celebratory party in a London restaurant.

He had been married since the week he finished his MBA in France. He looked so young at his wedding although he was twenty five years old. Suzanne, his wife had lived in our home for a year whilst Theo was studying in France.

She was an elegant bride and had become so slender in the weeks before her wedding. I made her special meals and followed her round with a big bottle of vitamins trying to build up her strength for the big day!

Theo was working long hours in the City and I worried about him. He seemed to be climbing the ladder of success very fast. He needed very little sleep which was a good job as he was at his desk before seven am every morning. He sometimes spent time in Europe and The States with his work.

One week got us tickets to see Paul McCartney at Earls Court which we loved. We had grown up with the Beatles and enjoyed the show tremendously. We had gone up to town on the train but it took us hours to get out of the stadium. As we were walking through the busy streets Grant had a brain wave.

Our youngest son James had just bought a flat in Pimlico and we thought he would come and pick us up. We rang his number and he was in bed as it was after midnight. When he answered the phone he could not believe his parents were out so late and proceeded to roundly remonstrate with us. We giggled as we waited at the side of the road.

We both collapsed into complete hysteria when we saw his grumpy face and could not believe we were being told off by the kid who we had waited outside myriad nightclubs and concerts for over the years.

Three new television programmes started this year. *BBC Breakfast* with its morning news round was popular with everybody.

I was not sure about Big Brother which seemed to involve staring at people as though they were animals in a clamorous zoo but I liked the *Wright Stuff* programme which was destined to run and run.

CHAPTER 10
Vancouver Sure Is A Beautiful City

You have not seen a tree until you have seen its shadow from the sky.
Amelia Earhart

I had been to Canada before but this was to be Grant's first visit and he was really looking forward to spending time there and seeing the family.

Our youngest son James had lived there for a year between school and university and I was very relieved when he came back home to us as I thought he might want to stay.

It is such an amazing place with wonderful people and I worried that he would like it so much that he would decide to stay there forever .The city of Vancouver is a coastal seaport with a population of about 600,000 people and spectacular views of the ocean and mountains.

Canada's population was about half that number when my three maternal aunts went to live there in 1957. Amy, Beth and Jane decided to go together and caused great consternation back home in Great Britain. My mother was one of eleven children and seven of her siblings were brothers. My grandmother Hester was a diminutive powerhouse but her children usually did as she commanded.

My youngest Aunt, Amy worked for a bank and was offered a two year secondment in Vancouver. She was single then but she went out and met her husband John the very day she arrived. My Aunt Jane was married to Jack but wanted an adventure and the third sister Beth and her husband Eric decided to join in the plan.

The journey on the plane was thirty hours and arduous but they all settled in quickly. Amy and John had married in Vancouver and had three children.

THE LOTUS GENERATION

Beth and her husband came back to England after two years bringing their small children with them.

Jane and her husband lived in England for a long time but finally settled on Vancouver Island.

I was looking forward to spending time with my Aunts, Uncles and cousins. They had an outdoor life with lots of excitement and adventure. They seemed to spend a lot less time commuting than we did in England. They spent those extra hours really enjoying life on the beach or skiing in Whistler.

We had been invited to stay in Vancouver with my cousin Joshua who was a lawyer. I had stayed at his house before and it was amazing. High ceilings and windows and a sweeping staircase that made you feel like a film star as you stepped carefully down it.

On our first morning we went for a walk in Stanley Park. This is my favourite park in the world, 1000 acres surrounded by the Pacific Ocean. The gardens are designed to bloom all year round and the cedar, fir and hemlock trees reach high into the sky.

The weather in Vancouver can sometimes be rainy which means that the rhododendron and azalea gardens are spectacular particularly from March to September. My favourite garden is the rose garden which was developed in 1920 and has roses of every colour and variety.

I love roses and when I see the different colours I am reminded of their meanings. Pink rose means grace, purple rose means enchantment, palest peach rose means modesty, red rose means love, orange rose means fascination and yellow raised means infidelity.

There is lots of first nation artwork to see including the totem pole display and some of the earlier examples were carved as early as 1880. The aquarium is world class and we walked around and saw the Orca whale.

This reminded me of the last time I was in Vancouver and took a light plane across to Vancouver Island. There was a pod of Orca whales leaping out of the ocean as we passed overhead. The black and white whales against the blue of the ocean were one of the most amazing sights I have ever seen. On my last visit I flew out alone and had a lot of fun but it rained on most days that I was there.

THE LOTUS GENERATION

On the only really sunny day I was waiting outside the supermarket for my aunts. Canadian supermarkets usually have rows of plants outside and I was admiring the fat, red geraniums as they came out of the store. At that moment gallons of freezing cold water sprayed over the plants and all over me. I screamed very loudly and the poor guy's face as he rushed round the stand was a picture.

My aunts collapsed with the giggles and everyone passing by joined in the merriment. I forced my frozen face into a smile and brushed my bedraggled hair out of my eyes. As I walked back to the car everything squelched loudly and that made my aunts laugh even more. I could honestly say that I had got wet every single day of my two week visit.

My Aunt Amy has a beautiful voice and I went with her to choir practise but after asking me to sing with the choir the first time they never mentioned it again.

My Aunt Jane had an elegant elderly neighbour with an apricot poodle. She baked delicious strawberry cake and had fascinating tales of her 1920s childhood in Alberta.

The second day of the visit we made a trip to the Okanagan Valley wine country. The views were absolutely amazing. The lush green foliage of the vines on the undulating fields is set off by the dark blue shades of the ever changing mountains. The 250 kilometre square area has distinct sub-regions which mean the changing soil and climate conditions can be home to merlot, pinot Gris, pinot noir and chardonnay grape vines.

We stopped for a delicious lunch of lamb with potato and fennel fricassee. We had a young pinot noir to drink and it matched perfectly. The waiter brought us ice cream and blueberries for dessert. There was also a plate of Nanaimo bars, British Columbia's favourite treat. I was very interested in these as we were headed for Nanaimo on Vancouver Island the next day.

After lunch we were taken round the winery and stopped to drink chocolate cups of ice wine. This is a dessert wine made from grapes frozen on the vine. The sugar dissolves but does not freeze and has to be pressed out. This results in a very concentrated sweet wine. Canada is one of the world's largest producers of ice wine.

CHAPTER 11
I Love The Island

A true traveller is he who goes on foot; even then he sits down a lot of the time.
Collette

We set off for a few days on Vancouver Island. The ferries run from Horse Shoe Bay to the Sunshine Coast where Aunt Amy had her holiday home. They run to Bowen Island where one of her children lived and to Nanaimo on Vancouver Island. The views from these ferries are spectacular with the Howe Sound in the background.

At Horse Shoe Bay there is a restaurant that sells the most delicious fish and chips. Whenever we left on a ferry journey we also built in an extra hour to partake of the soft, succulent white fish encased in glistening, golden batter and crunchy salty chips. As we waited in the queue amongst all the other travellers the expectation was heightened by the aromatic, all-encompassing scent that assailed the senses. There is nothing quite like the smell of sea air and crisp fish and chips to put a huge smile on people's faces.

Your sense of smell is the most powerful one that is linked to memory. When your olfactory receptors are stimulated they send powerful impulses to your brain. This is directly linked to your limbic system which is the part of your brain that deals with your emotions. The smell of new mown grass may take you back to childhood. The smell of Ponds cold cream immediately conjures up my Grandmother Hester. I am back in her bedroom with its high bedstead and the pink crochet bedspread where I could weave my small fingers in and out. When I close my eyes I can see her bedside cabinet with the tissues, cough drops and ubiquitous glass of warm orange squash.

I have always used two completely different perfumes in my life for completely different occasions .They are anchors for where I want to be at any particular time, whether the occasion is business or social. The only time I do not wear perfume is when there is a new baby in the family!

My first perfume is "Le Aire de Temps" by Nina Richie. Flowery with top notes of rose, bergamot, peach, neroli and carnation. Eleven year old Sophie, the very first French exchange visitor we ever

THE LOTUS GENERATION

had, brought me this as a thank you present from her Maman. Just holding the glass bottle with the white dove on top makes me relax and as I press the nozzle the cloud of sweet smelling mist reminds me of family, relaxation and home.

The other favourite perfume is "Opium" by Yves Saint Laurent. This one is spicy with top notes of mandarin orange, jasmine, bergamot and lily of the valley. I have worn this scent since I was in my twenties, when Grant bought it for me on our first wedding anniversary.

To me it says "Go get them girl". It is my anchor for power and is as important to me as my high heels, business clothes and perfectly groomed hair. I spray this delicious scent in front of me, walk through it and I am ready to meet any challenge.

I was leaning on the rail of the ferry admiring the ever-changing view when I suddenly felt myself being enveloped in a huge bear hug. I must admit I was a little startled as I had been miles away soaking in the atmosphere. I looked up into the deep blue eyes of a young cousin who I had not seen for a couple of years. He had been 5' 4" then and he was at least 6' 4" now and was very much a man with a faint fuzz of beard.

"Oh hello, Graham" I said "How are you and isn't this a glorious view". He fixed me with his seventeen year old gaze and said quizzically "What use is a view?"

I did not have an answer for him then and I do not have one now except that teenager's brains are just wired differently to the rest of us.

My Aunt Jane and Uncle Jack met us at the terminal and welcomed us to their home in Qualicum Beach. Their house was newly built in the open plan style with an American kitchen. Aunt Jane has exquisite interior design skills and every corner had a treat for the senses. A Lalique vase held a bunch of lilac roses and a perfect Persian rug from their home in England took pride of place in their dining room. I had always been very close to them and was looking forward to our visit. I knew there were lots to experience on Vancouver Island.

Qualicum Beach is on the Nanaimo lowlands which lie between the Georgia Basin and Vancouver Islands Ranges to the south. It was established in 1943 as a village and had grown to a town of 8000 people since then. The beautiful beach and stunning scenery means that it is a popular tourist resort in the summer. In the surrounding countryside there are black-tailed deer, Roosevelt elk, black bear, cougars and racoons.

Jane and Jack are very active retirees and by 7.30 am each day they were dressed and ready for the next adventure. We went hiking in the mountains, to tai chi lessons, played golf and ate at some wonderful restaurants.

On the last day of our time with them we had a drive to Victoria, the capital of Vancouver Island. The British Columbia Parliament buildings are located there and the baroque architecture is breath taking. Government house is located next to the botanical gardens and we had a tour of both places we had a really fun time with them and it was hard to say farewell.

Jane and Jack had lived with Grant and I for six months after they had sold their UK business and could not decide whether to stay or go back to Canada. We got home from work one day and they had decided to go back to Canada and they left the next day. I had always worried about whether they had made the right choice but seeing how happy they were set my mind at rest.

They took us to the ferry and we went back to Vancouver. Amy and John were there to meet us and we visited Granville Island with its mix of quaint shops, cafes and book stores. There is a definite feel good factor as there lots of street musicians playing everything from jazz to hip hop in the sunshine.

CHAPTER 12
The Dragon Racers

True fruit of travel is perhaps the feeling of being nearly everywhere at home.
Freya Stark

We had an early night as we were heading into the country to Kelowna for a few days. Amy's youngest daughter Sienna was competing in a dragon boat race and we were going to cheer her on.

THE LOTUS GENERATION

The next morning dawned hazy and warm and we were in good spirits as we left the house. John was the designated driver for the first part of the four hour trip. We were headed for Kelowna in the Okanagan region. We travelled through some amazing countryside and stopped for a delicious lunch. We all chose chowder served in hollowed out loaves of bread. The chowder was delicious with crispy bacon and cracker topping and I was delighted to find that the recipe was on the back of the menu.

We were soon on our way through fruit tree heaven. Cherries, Apricots, Peaches, Plums and Pears are all grown in this fertile land. Grant was driving as we turned into the circular driveway of the large house that we were staying in that night. As the others climbed out of the SUV to stretch their legs he looked back and me and raised his eyebrows. "Here we go again," he said in a polite but resigned tone.

Grant and I did not squabble about many things but "bed and breakfast" was one of the things we enjoyed disagreeing on. I loved staying in people's homes, learning about their lives and picking up local information. I thought hotels cold and impersonal. He loved cold, impersonal hotels where nobody bothered you. He hated "bed and breakfast" where you were invited to listen carefully to the story of the host's homes before being allowed in your room.

We were greeted at the door by the elegant Austrian couple who owned the property. The lady of the house took Amy and John left up some stairs and the gentleman put his hand out to indicate that we should go right.

Our first port of call was the bathroom which was outside our bedroom in the hall. The husband spent ten minutes describing the intricacies of the window which was only to be opened at certain times of the day. I was standing behind Grant and I am sure I saw steam coming out of his ears. The finicky man just droned on and on about all the rules that were to be obeyed. We just kept nodding our heads and smiling.

Eventually we were shown into our room and with a rider that we should only put our suitcase on the stand, never on the floor, he left us in peace.

The room was lovely and decorated in Tyrolean style. Shutters covered the window and when we looked out there were marvellous views of the garden. I lay down on the squashy feather bed decorated with a colourful quilt and was soon snoring.

Grant gently shook me awake and said softly "Time to go for a walk in the gardens," I slowly stood upright and realised with pleasure that the golden sun was setting in the west. I pulled on a little cashmere cardigan and headed outside. Emily, the wife, took us on a tour of her beautiful garden. She said "I spend every spare minute out here."

"I don't wonder she does, with a husband like him" Grant whispered in my ear as the others strolled ahead. I gave him my best tight lipped smiling frown. The one that signals, "Don't you dare say another word."

CHAPTER 13
The Borage Flowers

The flaming rose gloomed swarthy red: the borage gleams more blue, and low white flowers with starry head, glimmer the rich dusk through.

George McDonald

The garden was spectacular as the misty rainfall and warm conditions provided the perfect environment for lush growth. Peonies, roses, lilies, lupins scabious, gladioli and lavender grew in profusion and she took justifiable pride in her skills as a gardener.

The maple trees that Canada is so famous for were dotted about and the star-shaped white flowers of the British Columbian dogwood sparkled in abundance. The herbs transfixed me most, for although she had lots I could name, there were many other varieties as well. I recognised parsley, thyme, rosemary and the borage with its bright blue flowers.

The next morning breakfast was served on a high terrace with a glorious view of the dark Blue Mountains. Emily came round with the fragrant coffee and we enjoyed looking at the marvellous views.

Jacob, as we had been invited to call him, arrived holding the breakfast tray aloft in one hand. He placed it down with a flourish and said firmly "Voila".

THE LOTUS GENERATION

As I looked across at his offered repast and I must admit it looked delicious. Eggs Benedict in all its glory covered four plates. There were toasted English muffins, a thick slice of local ham, a gently quivering poached egg and shiny hollandaise sauce covering it all in a smooth blanket of yellow.

That would have been enough for anybody to set them up for the day. Except the breakfast was not the only thing on the plate, there was also an artfully arranged sprinkling of bright blue borage flowers covering everything.

Jacob fixed my husband with his gaze and said clearly so that there could be no mistake. "You must eat a borage flower with every mouthful to get the full flavour experience" Although Grant does not care for bed and breakfast establishments, like most men he absolutely loathes being told what to do.

"No thank you" my husband said quietly. "I must insist" said Jacob.

"No thank you," said Grant a little more firmly.

"Nobody has ever refused to eat the borage flowers in the ten years I have been offering them" said Jacob.

"No thank you," said Grant in a very determined voice. Everyone on the terrace had stopped mid mouthful and was staring.

Suddenly a man with a pronounced Scots Canadian accent said "Well, you know, I have tried one and I am completely sure that I am never going to eat another one." Everyone smiled as the ice was broken. Jacob turned on his heel and went back to the kitchen.

I must admit I was more than a little put out by my husband refusing the borage flowers. I thought that politeness dictated that he should have tried one. However I agreed with myself that if I ever ran any kind of hostelry in the future I would not insist that anybody ate anything they did not want.

We arrived just in time to see the start of the dragon boat racing. I could see my cousin Sienna's pale blonde hair bobbing about on her team's watercraft. Dragon boats are human powered and they were all decorated with Chinese Dragon heads and tails. This was to show that this was a major competition.

The colours of the heads were powerful shades of vibrant red, ochre yellow and emerald green. People standing near us explained that different coloured dragons have different meanings. A gold dragon means wealth and wisdom, a black dragon means storms and winter and the imperial yellow dragon means the centre of the earth.

We counted the crew on each boat and it appeared to be twenty two plus a drummer. The drummers were seated at the centre of the boats so that they could be heard above the roar. There was also a sweeper sitting at the back of each boat that steered the craft. The drum beat from each boat synchronised to make a very hypnotic sound that resounded in our chests. The excitement in the crowd grew and they all surged forward.

A sharp shot rang through the air and the boats were off and so were the blue jays out of the trees. They flew into air with a huge squawk and the floated back down like so many deflated plastic bags. We shouted and cheered for Sienna's team as they flew along the lake.

There were hundreds of people surrounding the shore picnicking and enjoying a day out in the fresh air. I looked around me and thought that the Canadians really know how to enjoy their beautiful country. Sienna's team won first prize in their race and there were many beaming faces that day in the sunshine.

` We had fun on the rest of our trip. We spent a few days on the Sunshine Coast in my Aunt's holiday home. Friends from their early married life were neighbours there. Everyone seemed to own a boat and the yacht club was the centre of their lives.

Eric and Barbara had been to Europe many times and whenever I saw him he always regaled me with the same joke. "When I go out walking I always carry a pair of trainers around my neck in case I see a grizzly bear."

Then I would say "Eric, you cannot out run a grizzly bear."

He would howl with laughter and then say "No, but I can out run Barbara".

The assembled company would fall about laughing. It worked every time.

During the last few days of our trip I went with Amy to see my Cousin Joanna's house on Bowen Island. She had a beautiful home in amongst the trees, right by the water's edge. In common with a lot of Canadian homes they lived on the first floor and slept downstairs in what they called the basement. This meant the views from their home were amazing. Their yacht bobbed about at the bottom of their garden and they used the ferry as though it was the local bus.

Accountants, shop owners, bus drivers and school children stood every morning in the queue with their coffee chatting away and walked up a ramp to their seats. The views from the ferries are utterly spectacular with an ever-changing colour palate. It seems to be a given that people get used to their surroundings, but I have never met anyone there who did not appreciate their glorious surroundings.

On the last day Joshua took Grant up in his light aircraft and showed him Vancouver from the air. Later on that day they went with John to watch the Vancouver Canucks hockey team. They travelled in Joshua's sports car and so he drove to the stadium. Grant offered to sit in the back of the Porsche as he was the smaller and younger than John.

I was in asleep when they got back and when he got in bed Grant woke me and said quietly "I really do not feel very well". I felt his head and he was not warm but as I put my arms around him I realised he was shivering ever so slightly.

We left the next day for England and I thought we were very lucky to have such an extraordinary family who made us so welcome.

CHAPTER 14
My Heart Hurts

Be thankful for every beat of your broken heart. For the pain is a reminder that you are alive and have the strength to move on.

Anon.

"Finally I can go to sleep" I thought to myself as I felt my body start to relax. I was in my own bed for the first time in weeks. I had loved my trip to Vancouver and had enjoyed being with my extended family. There is something about being with your aunts and uncles that make you feel childlike no matter how old you are.

We arrived back early that morning and spent the day enjoying that cosy feeling of being in your own home. I was so pleased to see our old golden retriever, Bella, as we had had her for a very long time. I loved coming down in the morning to see her face so delighted to see me or anybody else for that matter! I was very lucky and I had her marvellous company for eighteen years apparently almost unheard of with a golden retriever.

Our oldest son Theo had rung to invite us out for supper and so we met him and his wife Suzanne at seven pm. My father was also with us at the restaurant. We showed photographs and exchanged good wishes from the extended family members.

We had a lovely meal and caught up on all the news from the three weeks we had been away. When we got home, father who lived with us yawned and said "I am off to bed; I have an early start in the morning". He was going up to the Lake District for a few days.

Grant insisted that he was going to watch some sport before bed and so I left him in the den watching television. I lay in bed and stretched out luxuriously. I had taken a sleeping tablet because I knew I had to rest because I had a busy week ahead. My mind would not quieten and so I did the thing I had always taught my children.

"Lie on your back and concentrate on your toes. Squeeze them and then relax them slowly. Move to your feet concentrate, squeeze and relax. Going up your body and the idea is that you are asleep before you reach your head."

I was just drifting off when my body was filled with a powerful shot of adrenaline and I sat bolt upright in the dark. Whatever was the matter? I waited a moment for my wildly beating heart to settle into a sensible rhythm.

My hand searched the pillow next to me and realised I was alone in bed. The sleeping draught started to lull me back into a state of slumber. I lay there for a few moments and thought "I better get up and check"

I felt a little woozy as I descended the staircase. I popped my head round the door of the den, the cricket was on but Grant was not there. The only other light that was on was the kitchen.

I shouted "please put the kettle on." Then I realised that I was calling into to an empty space...

The door from the kitchen to the utility room was slightly ajar and I went across to close it. The adjoining garage was in darkness but I could make out a strange shape on the floor behind the car. I flicked the light switch and stared in horror.

There is a thing that happens when something traumatic occurs; time seems to stretch out and hover before you going on and on into the distance. It seemed to take me forever to reach him. His face was the colour of putty under the harsh glare of the florescent lights. He was lying on his side with this hands clasped across his chest.

As I felt for his pulse I realised he was still conscious. "I really feel very ill" he whispered "I have a pain under my arm." I kissed him on the forehead and told him he would be alright. I ran back into the kitchen. I skidded to a stop because I knew I was panicking.

"Think, think. Think" I told myself "Should I drive him in the car, should I summon the doctor?" "No" said my mind "Dial 999."

I explained the situation to the operator and then ran to get a pillow and a blanket from the kitchen sofa. When I got back to him he was still on his side, unconscious but thankfully breathing and so I made him as comfortable as I could. I made sure that his airway was clear and then went to open the front door for the paramedics.

It was exactly seven minutes when the dark night was filled with the deep blue of flashing lights. A man and a woman in paramedic uniforms ran straight through the front door firing questions at me. How old was he? How long since this had happened? The rest just faded into a blur. I could not move forward or backwards until they finally said "We have him stabilised enough to take him to hospital."

They wanted to take him out to the ambulance on a stretcher but there were cars parked on the drive. I collected the car keys and began moving cars until only one remained. That of course was the one blocking the front door. My son James had gone back to University leaving his car but I had no idea where the key had been stored.

Eventually the paramedics managed to get him out of the French windows, over the rockery and down the garden path. I did think, even through my tears that it looked more like an episode of "Some Mothers Do have 'Em" rather than a serious attempt to get a heart attack patient to hospital. As I bent to kiss him as they put in the ambulance, I realised he was awake and staring at me under his oxygen mask. I told him I loved him and squeezed his hand before I jumped into the car to follow him the mile to the local hospital.

CHAPTER 15
The Frontal Cortex Is Vital To Judgement

I wrote your name on the sand and it washed away, I wrote it in the air and it blew away, I wrote it on my heart and it got broken.

Anon.

I said a silent prayer and squeezed the tears from my eyes. I could not lose him; I had loved him absolutely since I was in my early teens.

I had read all the books that tell you that early state of intoxication does not last as it is replaced by something less heady but more constant. When we fall in love, we are told, it makes us crazy and we could not live life in that traumatic state.

Scientists have mapped the chemical changes that happen when we fall in love. Certain parts of the brain activate and others shut down when we are in that blissful state. The frontal cortex is vital to judgement and shuts down when we are in that early phase and so when being in love is replaced by falling in love, then reason and judgment return.

After all these years I was still trapped in that early phase of falling in love when reasoned judgement disappears. Whenever I saw him my heart started beating wildly and being with him made me euphoric. However I had always known that he did not love me as I loved him.

My marriage had been a roller coaster to say the least. I said to him on our wedding day "I will always love you and stay married to you no matter what you do" and he had taken me at my word.

A friend once told me "The only kind of being in love that lasts a lifetime is the unrequited kind." She laughed as she said "Don't quote me but I think it's a Woody Allen bon mot" I raised my eyebrows and thought what I know, "My judgment has been definitely impaired all my married life".

I imagined that Grant must have had a heart attack as we drove behind the ambulance. My father had been wakened by the noise and had agreed to drive me as I was shaking so much. I held my hands together tightly to stop them shaking and offered a prayer for his recovery.

THE LOTUS GENERATION

I had been on enough first aid courses to recognise the symptoms. Grant was fifty-one years old and very slim and fit but he had had a lot of ups and downs in the ten years since he had left his career in the oil industry.

I rang my son Theo who lived near us and he met us at the hospital. Miranda was on an extended visit to Australia and James was away at University. Grant was touch and go through the night. I was questioned closely about his medical history and they took copious notes. However once they realised he had just stepped off a long haul flight they insisted on treating him for a thrombosis.

He was in hospital for two weeks being treated with warfarin and I kept asking if this could have been a heart attack. The answer from every doctor was negative. When I tried to marshal my thoughts enough to form a cogent argument I was met with a shake of the head. The weather turned cold and snowy in November and Grant stayed home most of the time.

He watched a lot of television which was unusual for him. A favourite was *Who wants to be a Millionaire?* especially when Judith Keppel was the first person to win £1,000,000. We knew that St James was the patron saint of Spain for £500,000 but we not sure about the million pound question.

"Which king was married to Eleanor of Aquitaine?" We argued over which Henry it was and it turned out to be the Henry II.

I had started to listen to music instead of Radio Four whilst cooking and ironing in the kitchen to try to lift my mood. I occasionally felt a primeval urge to embark on Tarantism or crazy dancing, to dispel my melancholic state. The fact that it was thought to be caused by a tarantula bite in sixteenth century Italy, stayed my feet.

I loved the sounds of the moment including Shania Twain, The Backstreet Boys, The Corrs and David Grey. Shania Twain's album *Come on Over* got a lot of airtime in my car.

The thought that I knew my husband was very ill but I could do nothing to help him recover caused me great anxiety.

December brought arctic weather conditions and the country was almost brought to a halt in -13 degree temperatures. We hosted a snowy Christmas but everyone was yearning for spring to arrive.

THE LOTUS GENERATION

It was six months and eleven hospital appointments later when they actually confirmed it was his heart that had been the problem. That was when they were wheeling him into theatre for an emergency quadruple bypass.

We had found a wonderful heart surgeon Mr Saab and Grant had his bypass operation in a small hospital near to our home. It was run by a religious order and so was very peaceful and calm. The chapel was a place of tranquillity and succour and I spent a lot of time in there with my own thoughts. The nun's grey habits swished as they passed and there was always a warm smile to enjoy and a hand to hold.

His bypass operation was started in the evening and so did not finish until midnight. Miranda and James sat with me throughout and I was glad of their support. James had come back from his skiing holiday and Miranda was back from Australia.

All I really remember from the surgeon's post-operative talk were his sage words. "He must walk, preferably uphill every day for the rest of his life:" He spent a week in hospital after the surgery and was understandably very subdued.

I went to collect him just after he had his staples out. He looked at me and said, "I really don't want to go home with you yet, I will just stay here for a few more days." I patted his hand and said tentatively, "OK, my love."

Our daughter Miranda was outside with the car. I went back through the doors and asked her to go and see if he would come out with her. Five minutes later she reappeared smiling with her Dad on her arm.

When we got home I helped him upstairs to the bedroom that I had so carefully prepared for him. His nightstand was filled with all the things an invalid would need, magazines, tissues, biscuits, drinks and books were within his reach.

We stood side by side in the bedroom doorway for a few minutes whilst he surveyed the scene. This spectral stranger with the dark eyes and grey beard eventually moved his gaze from the floor to look at me. After a while he said, "You do realise that if I get in bed I will never get out again don't you".

I nodded my head and we went back downstairs, slow and doddering. Then I made a delicious lunch which he ate sparingly. I asked him if he was in pain. "Yes" he said "Where?" I replied. He took a few moments and then said "Inside and outside, actually."

CHAPTER 16
What A Lovely Visit To Cornwall

Travel is as much a passion as ambition or love
L.E.Landon

Grant was feeling much better. He had started to attend a recuperation clinic at the local hospital and being with other bypass patients had been beneficial to his recovery. One morning a letter arrived with a booking for us to spend a week in Cornwall at a Rick Stein's hotel and restaurant. Our son Theo had arranged it for us and we were really pleased.

My father Murray, who was in his early seventies, was back from his visit north but our life was no longer the pedestrian routine that it had been since he came to live with us. I had been working from home and I used to have my lunch with him most days and we would pit our wits as we did the crossword.

I suppose he had been the focus of most of my attention for some years but now my husband needed me much more.

I really did not think too much about this at that time. We still had lovely meals together and did all the other things that you do as a family. However my father was no longer the most important person in my life and I felt that very keenly but I did not have any other choice. I was just glad my husband was still alive and well but things had definitely changed in our house.

I asked father if he would look after the dogs and we set off on our trip to Cornwall. I was the designated driver as Grant had not had the all clear from the hospital. The roads were still empty enough for the trip to be enjoyable.

When we arrived in Padstow we found The Rick Stein hotel easily. The hotel room was stylish and comfortable and the food we had there was exquisite. We had oyster's charentaise, hot spicy

THE LOTUS GENERATION

sausage with cold oysters, ragout of brill and scallop, seafood dieppoise to name a few dishes, all absolutely delicious.

We strolled every day along the beaches near Padstow. The weather was warm and there were very few people about. We walked for long distances but I was sure to keep my phone with me in case of emergency. We reminisced and laughed about the first mobile phone he ever had with the enormous battery pack. I was so pleased he could walk so far but I did not try to coax him to walk uphill as the rocks seemed very slippery.

The Eden Project was an amazing experience. As we waited in the queue the height of the domes dominates the environment. The two huge enclosures look like something from outer space. They are joined together and house thousands of plant species from around the world. Steel frames support hundreds hexagonal and pentagonal inflated plastic cells. As we waited in the queue to go into the entrance the sun began to shine and I collected a tan that was to last me all summer.

Once you are inside the size of the place is just breathtaking. If you look up at the trees you can see an eclectic mix including bamboo, cacao, macadamia and fig. The climbers scatter their amazing jewel like colours around and about, wherever your eyes wander. The Jade vine plants were weaving in and out of the trees giving a cooling green background to the hot pink of the bougainvillea and Chilean bellflower. The scent of vanilla and hops hovers in the steamy air.

If you looked down there were orchids, dahlias, aloe and water lilies carpeted the ground as far as the eye can see. We did not stay very long as the patient was feeling tired and a little breathless but it was an amazing experience none the less.

Our visit to the lost Gardens of Heligan was the most memorable day of the whole trip. With sandwiches and drinks secreted about our persons we took the whole day to wander as there were plenty of stopping places for a rest.

The gardens are at Mevagissey and were neglected after the First World War. This allowed the rhododendrons and camellias to grow to a colossal size. I remember watching the television programme in the 1990s about the restoration but nothing prepares you for the sheer scale of the undertaking.

My favourite place is the walled garden. The sun was shining as we arrived there and the warmth of the walls made it a magical place to sit and reflect how lucky we were that Grant had come through this unscathed.

As we packed our bags and headed for the car a little shiver passed through me and I looked up to see a black cloud passing the sun. I wondered if this was a metaphor for the next phase of my life. I knew I could not please everyone and when the thought crossed my mind I knew I should make a plan that included my welfare. Then the thought flew away like a will- o'- the- wisp and I did not think about it until lots of heartache later.

When we arrived home we settled into a routine and our life seemed definitely smaller and greyer than it had been before. I was looking after my demanding father and had a husband who seemed, understandably to have lost his zest for life.

Grant had had two serious spells of depression in his adult life and I ran around trying to keep his muddled grey state from floating towards the black morass from which I could not pull him back. It took every ounce of effort to keep everything on an even keel. I was still on extended leave from work but I knew my physical shape was not good and I was still walking with a cane at this time because of my MS.

The Labour Party won that summer's general election and William Hague resigned as Leader of the Opposition. He had been a precocious talent for the Tory party since speaking at their conference when he was just sixteen. I had always admired his intellect and found him to be a clear and concise speaker at Question Time.

I looked at myself in the mirror one misty, mournful morning and stared critically at my reflection and several things crossed my mind. "Get on with it girl, you can't be young forever but you can be modern and remain excited about life," then "I definitely need some highlights" and most of all "I would really, really love a grandchild."

CHAPTER 17
The Day Of The Decision

I love to feel blonde all over.
Marilyn Monroe

The shiny black gown was far too tight around my neck and very, very itchy. I wiggled this way and that to make myself more comfortable and nothing was working. I could feel my breathing becoming more laboured. With a big sigh I stood up and tried to rearrange the slippery tent.

"Are you alright there," said Paul as he put a cup of fragrant coffee, on the shelf, in front of me. I smiled weakly and caught a glimpse of my reflection in the mirror. I was a brunette with very dark eyebrows that were set in a frown. In fact I thought like a brunette and I dressed like a brunette. I had been a brunette forever as I was born with a shock of jet black hair and a dark mono brow that made me looks like Frida Kahlo, the Mexican painter.

The trouble was that it was taking more and more time and effort just to keep my own colour. My right side parting had become my mortal enemy with a mind of its own. I went to bed looking fine and woke up looking like an old lady... It was as if a malevolent fairy had taken a paint brush and pot of white paint and dabbed it artfully on my parting overnight.

A week after I had it coloured the whole thing it seemed determined to revert to a whiter shade of pale. I was back working by then as trainer and presenter and would find myself in front of large groups of people explaining serious government policy. I would feel business like and competent and then I would see my reflection and be plunged back to being the lady with the grey parting. I hoped she only existed in my head but the time had come to do something about it. My patina of elegance and pulchritude appeared to be deserting me.

Paul, my hairdresser had persuaded me that blonde was the way forward. I trusted him implicitly as he had done my hair for years but I had not mentioned this change to anyone else. He set about the transformation and it took a few hours during which I kept my eyes firmly closed.

THE LOTUS GENERATION

When I finally looked in the mirror the person looking back was definitely not me. I had started with a dark brown bob and now had a head of blonde hair that frankly went this way and that. Paul had got carried away and decided to add a few layers as he went along. He was so pleased with his handiwork that I paid him and wished him a fond adieu.

It was only when I left the hairdressers that I looked down. I had gone there straight from the gym and was wearing leggings, trainers and a fitted top. I caught sight of myself in the butcher's window and thought I looked frankly crackers! The butcher waved cheerily and I am ashamed to say I put my head down and ignored him. I drove the half a mile home thinking to myself "Thank goodness nobody is home"

As I rounded the corner I noticed my daughter Miranda's car on the drive. She had just pulled up and was getting out of her car. She took one look and burst into peals of laughter. "Come on in Maggie-lo, I will make you a cup of tea" she chuckled as she opened the door with her key.

"Maggie-lo, Maggie-lo who on earth is that?" I cried. She looked at me with tears of mirth in her eyes. "You look like Maggie Thatcher on the top half and Jennifer Lopez on the bottom half.

I glanced in the hall mirror and had to agree.

It took me about three months to get used to being a blonde. None of my clothes looked right. I had always worn a lot of black for the office and pinks, reds and purples made me who I was in my home life.

Nothing looked right so I thought about my mother Mona who had been a life long blonde. Slowly I started to wear navy instead of black and softer blues and greens instead of purples and bright pinks.

The eternal question crossed my mind. "Do blondes have more fun?" Well, I am absolutely convinced that traffic stops more regularly when you are blonde.

However I really could not answer with any certainty because in my head I was still a brunette. If I ever passed a mirror and caught sight of myself I gave a little start!

CHAPTER 18
The News We Have Waited For

I have been godmother loads of times but being a grandmother is better than anything.

Vivien Leigh

Finally the news I had been waiting for, our daughter was having a baby. When she rang to tell us the news Grant and I danced around the kitchen with glee. When we stopped twirling I realised we were still holding each other close. I looked into his eyes and realised we had not done that for a long time.

Then a thought arrived unbidden and my solar plexus was tight with a tension. I realised that I had been so busy studying, working and looking after all these people that I had forgotten my husband.

I could not remember the last time we had been out together or even talked. That night we went out to dinner and talked about everything including the excitement of becoming grandparents. We did not know how we were going to manage to wait another seven months for this darling baby to arrive.

I was sitting with my father watching the television early one autumn morning. The mellow sunlight streamed through the sitting room window and bounced off my grandmother's antique Lalique vase on the window ledge. My father loved the news and very often postulated his opinion for discussion. On that beautiful morning I sat down with him to have our coffee.

I was not aware of the date but was to remember it later. On September 11th 2001 two planes were flown into the twin towers at the World Trade Centre in New York. Another plane was flown into the Pentagon. It was deemed to be a terrorist attack by al Qaeda led by Osama Bin Laden. Over 3000 people were killed that day in the most horrendous of circumstances

Along with many other people we stared blindly at the television for many hours unable to believe what we were seeing. A paroxysm of profound sadness and pain filled our hearts for months afterwards. The ramifications of that terrible day shaped the next decade and onwards.

THE LOTUS GENERATION

Not long after we got this terrible news father suddenly turned to me and with a rueful expression said "I have been thinking about this and I am going to move back up North."

I felt very shocked and saddened as there had been absolutely no discussion of this before and I asked him why ever he would want to leave us. He had always been a very impulsive man with a quixotic streak but this was extreme even for him. Once he got a notion in his mind he just followed it through without thought for the consequences.

Mother had kept him in check with humour and determination but since she died he had been impossible. He was such good fun most of the time but you really never knew what was coming next.

The summer after my mother died I had gone to stay with him for a few weeks. He had moved to a bungalow in a Lakeland village with a small but pleasant back garden.

There was a twelve foot tall conifer hedge at the end of the patio and I had no idea what was on the other side.

One day I asked him what he wanted for supper and in the time it took me to make a ham salad he had rushed into the shed, picked up the chain saw he had used on his previous large garden and demolished the conifer hedge completely.

I went back outside with a tray laid for two. It was only to find an elderly single lady standing with her head in her hands and her mouth shaped in a silent Edward Munch scream.

I quickly recognised her, as years before she had taught at a primary school where I had been a governor. She had planted the hedge twenty years before and she was inconsolable at the sight of her ravaged vegetable garden. I ran round to help her and next morning a local carpentry company came and restored her privacy with a large expensive oak fence that father had to pay for.

Whilst father lived with us we had had a lot of good times but I had also come home to find the back door cut in half, my precious blue conifers by the front door dug up and my washing machine at the tip because the door catch was faulty.

He had spent nearly six years and done so many things whilst living with us. He had been there for the children's graduations and weddings. He loved the parties and the good times but found daily life boring and was always looking for the next excitement.

My friends invited him to dinner and introduced him to new people but nothing was ever enough. I really hoped he would meet someone as he loved to travel but he hated being on his own.

He moved house many times after he left us, always searching for the next adventure.

I knew I would miss him terribly. He had a circle of friends from the bridge club but no one could replace my mother in his life. I knew he felt that he had lost first place in my affections since Grant had been ill. I also knew that the news that there was a grandchild on the way meant that he thought that he would definitely get less attention.

I wondered if he would think about living in Canada as he spent so much time there but he wanted to go back to Manchester where he had been happiest. He was still in his seventies and fitter than I was, so I did not worry for his welfare.

I was terribly upset to lose him and felt really that he would be better staying with us but there was no changing his mind. One of the last things my mother had whispered to me was "Make sure that you take good care of your father" and I really did not know whether she meant that it was to be a forever promise as I tossed and turned each night away.

I dreaded the day he went, but the sadness diminished and I was left with a feeling of guilt that pervaded everything. I knew in my head he was fine but over the next few weeks I felt that I had really let my mother down. I tried to view it logically and as I sat looking out of the window a perfect truth came to me.

"No matter how old you are now, if you live with a parent then you are always a child". I decided there and then that I would try never to put that pressure on my own children.

I spent hours in the next few months talking to my father on the phone but I must admit I felt younger and freer without his constant presence. I renovated the house and spent many happy hours in my wonderful garden. Shopping for baby clothes was delightful and soon it was summer and the arrival was imminent.

Then many years later father eventually met the wonderful Stella, who recently widowed, walked into his life when he was least expecting it. It is lovely to see him with someone who shares his life so completely.

CHAPTER 19
The Baby Has Arrived

The best birthdays of all are those that have not arrived yet.
Anon.

My daughter had been really well during her pregnancy. My greatest fear was that she would have the terrible sickness that I had suffered throughout all my pregnancies. *Hyperemesis Gravidarium* had meant that I was sick from being a week pregnant until the day I gave birth, but my fears were unfounded and she was really well throughout the whole nine months.

My granddaughter was due on my birthday. Grant, Miranda and I went out to have a celebratory tapas lunch. The restaurant was bright and airy with a fantastic fountain outside. It was a perfect day and Miranda looked so radiant in her royal blue linen dress.

We sat for two hours in the restaurant enjoying the food and the atmosphere. Miranda and I walked arm in arm out of the restaurant whilst Grant paid the bill.

"Ooh" said Miranda and sat down on the edge of the waterfall. "What?" said I with rising alarm?

"Oooh!" said Miranda as her Dad walked up to us "That lunch has not agreed with me, Oooh!"

It took us a little while to convince her that as this was the day her daughter was due, and then it might be the start of her imminent arrival. We rang her husband and agreed to meet him back at their house.

I left my daughter at her London home, well on into her labour and said " I will see you at the hospital later on darling," Alistair, my son-in-law in a very determined voice and said to me, " Go home and wait, I will ring you and let you know as soon as there is something to tell you."

THE LOTUS GENERATION

They had made a decision that they wanted to do this alone and I had to respect that.

We set off home to wait and worry. We waited and waited and the long day turned into an excruciating night. The night went by minute by minute, with endless cups of tea and desultory pointless conversations. As dawn broke Grant said to me "Come on we are going out for a walk and then there is an auction on today in Dorking, where we can buy something for the baby".

The mist was rolling over the downs and the summer air was still crisp and chill as we set off on our dawn constitutional. Our elderly golden retreiver walked in front but kept glancing back for reassurance. As we passed the stables she lagged behind us but we were too engrossed in our concerned conversation to notice.

Bella, the golden retriever, did not very often run these days but when she got an idea in her mind she was capable of great bursts of speed. We were walking on a narrow path to the woods with our heads together, in our own reverie, when we were both knocked to the ground. Bella had picked a long stick, put on a burst of speed and knocked us both right in the back of the knees consequently we went down like nine pins!

She loved the fact that we were both on the ground with her and began barking excitedly and licking our faces. We had to laugh as we helped each other up but the episode broke our sombre mood. We were very worried about our daughter but moping about was not going to help her. Babies take their own time to arrive, they always have done and they always will do.

We hurried back to the house and had croissants and coffee and then drove to the auction. We had decided that a desk would be an appropriate gift and were delighted to see a darling rosewood example which would be perfect.

I love the auction house and picked up my number at the door. I looked around and the all regulars were there. In the front seats the couples that loved a day out. Further back the people who had their eye on a particular piece and at the back the professionals who wanted a bargain.

THE LOTUS GENERATION

We decided early on what we wanted to pay but fortunately there was only one other bidder who dropped out quickly and soon we were the proud owners of a rosewood desk.

We headed home and realised we had only been waiting twenty seven hours and we must be patient. About eight pm the phone rang. It was our son James who said, "I cannot take any more waiting!" We assured him that we would let him know the minute we knew. Five minutes later the phone rang again and we both rushed to answer it but it was my sister Gillian "I cannot take any more waiting" We assured her we would let her know the minute we knew any news. We sat staring at each other as the long minutes went slowly by as we became more and more inactive.

The bell on the phone rang out like a shot into the silent space between us. We clambered on heavy limbs towards the phone. I got there first and finally heard the words I had been waiting for. "Your granddaughter is safe in the world and your daughter is doing fine after a very long labour" Our son-in-law sounded exhausted and elated in the mix of emotions only available to a new father.

I did not say goodbye because I was already in the car on the way to meet the newest member of the family. There is no more profound feeling than your first grandchild in your arms. I was gazing at her in awe when I looked across at my exhausted daughter and my heart went out to her.

As a mother your first instinct is to make your daughter's life painless and perfect but this is one assignment you cannot help her with.

CHAPTER 20
We Are Chasing Around Henry Moore

To know one thing, you must know the opposite.
Henry Moore

We spent many happy days; just the three of us girls after Ellie was born. A lot of these days were spent at the majestic Wisley Gardens which are the headquarters of the Royal Horticultural Society. You can have a different experience every time you visit the nearly two hundred acres of gardens.

THE LOTUS GENERATION

There is a different scene depending on the time of year but it is especially wonderful in spring. As you walk up the hill and view the magnolias, azaleas and rhododendrons in all their glory you will discover a perfect stimulus for the senses. The sight of all the shades of pink and white and lilac stuns you. When you stop to take in all the visual magic you will be overpowered by the exquisitely sweet and heady fragrance of the magnolia trees which is like nothing else on earth.

The magnolia tree in all its varieties is bare and cold in winter but as spring erupted the flower buds stood firm and proud away from the wizened branches. If you stop and gaze into the tulip-shaped pale cream flower you will delighted by its pale pink centre. You need to take advantage though, of a warm spring day as one cruel frost or windstorm and the whole thing disappears in a moment.

The camellia in all its shades of pink and red is a relative of the tea plant from Asia. Mostly grown in pots in domestic gardens these delightful plants grow large and luxurious at Wisley.

The high domed rhododendrons are the stars of the show on Battleston hill. Standing taller than a man in all shades of pink, red, purple and white they form perfect cover for a small child's game of hide and seek.

The azaleas are smaller but the flowers are exquisitely formed and they look spectacular amongst the higher trees. Their colour palate includes a lemony yellow as well as all the colours in the red and pink spectrum.

The hill includes lots of spring planting, jonquils, daffodils, tulips and fragrant hyacinths that have you kneeling to catch the scent.

At the top of Battleston Hill stands a mammoth Henry Moore sculpture that proves impossible for tiny fingers to resist. Wisley also run wonderful evenings under the stars to be enjoyed by an excited audience.

With my dear friend Lynn and her sister-in-law Joan we went to hear the tenor Russell Watson. We arrived early equipped with beach chairs, picnic rugs, champagne and lots of wonderful things to eat. As we were early we managed to sit right near the front. Grant assembled all our seats in a very gentlemanly manner and remarked to me

THE LOTUS GENERATION

quietly that he was afraid that our chairs were a little sturdier than theirs.

Lots of fans came up and sat on the grass in front of us but that was fine because we were still near the stage. Russell Watson was just perfect and it was one of the best nights of music that I had the privilege of attending.

I was a little perplexed at one point as I turned to give Lynn her glass of champagne and realised she had disappeared from beside me. As I looked this way and that there was a small, strangled sob and I realised the legs from her chair had slowly sunk down and had disappeared down into the damp grass. Lynn is seven inches shorter than me anyway so she was actually positioned with her head just under my left elbow. I laughed so loudly that the champagne went up my nose. As I sat coughing, spluttering and giggling I could hear the assembled company telling me to "shhh". I am sure the star of the show caught my gaze as well.

A couple of weeks later Grant arrived home with tickets to see his favourite group The Hollies. We decided to get there early again and the same thing happened, crowds of fans sat down in front of us. Grant remarked that we would be fine as we had a good seat two weeks before.

I must admit that I could take or leave the Hollies but I liked the Searchers who were on the bill with them. As soon as the music started I realised something that I should never have forgotten, that older people like to get up and dance too. Within seconds of the music starting we were surrounded by jiggling bottoms in our eye line and a lot of shouting and shoving was going on. Grant said, "We are going to have to stand up, love," and hauled me to my feet. I actually had quite high heels on so they pinioned me and I was forced to dance rooted to the spot with the back of my legs pushed into my sturdy, sharp beach chair.

The pain was shooting up and down my trapped legs as the music stopped and I was grateful to sit down. Early middle age was definitely upon me and advancing.

Minutes later The Hollies came on and as I gave them a desultory glance until I realised that my favourite singer from my youth, Carl Wayne was leading the band out.

THE LOTUS GENERATION

I leapt to my feet as he began to sing *Flowers in the Rain* from his Move days and I was completely entranced. I remember listening to that song in 1967 as Tony Blackburn's Radio One show first hit the airways.

I kicked off my shoes and danced for the next two hours to every Hollies and Move song they sang. It was a magical evening, never to be forgotten even if Grant had to carry me back to the car.

I still keep my Wisley membership current to this day even if I only use it a couple of times a year.

CHAPTER 21
New York Here We Come

The most interesting New Yorkers are the people who were not born there.
Elaine Stritch

I had just been to Waitrose and as I walked back in the kitchen the phone was ringing. It was my sister Gillian, who I had not seen for a few months. What she said next absolutely amazed me.

"Hi love, I have been thinking that I really want to go to New York to do some shopping, so I have booked you a ticket to come with me". "Wow," I thought. Although I had spent a lot of time on the west coast of America I had never been to New York and so this was really exciting news. My niece Claire who was just about to get married was coming with us, but my granddaughter Ellie was too young for my daughter Miranda to leave for a few days.

We met at the airport and the flight was on time. I had always had a problem with long haul flights as I just could not sleep but I had enough books to keep me occupied.

As with all famous places, from the cinema and television, New York seemed very familiar on the ride from the airport to Times Square. We checked into the hotel and there were two queen sized beds in the room which was on the 52nd floor.

I had looked after my niece Claire, when she was very small, when my sister had gone back to work. The result of those early years was that we were still very close.

However that darling little girl with the curls and the beautiful green eyes had been superseded by a very business-like management consultant. When she looked at the two beds she said very firmly "Well, you two will just have to share a bed!" And neither her mother nor her aunt was prepared to disagree.

The first restaurant that we came to on our evening walk was a lobster and steak restaurant. We peered into the brightly lit window and it seemed very cheery and full of bonhomie so we went inside. Our blonde waiter showed us to our table with just a scintilla of distain and two minutes later reappeared with a paper bib which he tied round my sister's neck.

He then went to tie one round my niece's neck. She put her hand out like a traffic policeman and said in her most formal received pronunciation "Do not even think about it, young man". She was all of twenty five years old.

He just shrugged and I just meekly allowed him to tie a paper bib around my neck with a word of complaint.

I had eaten lobster before, particularly in San Francisco and this specimen was a very poor relation but we all smiled and paid the bill without comment remembering to leave the right percentage tip. We got back to our bedroom which was distinctly chilly as it was very cold outside.

Grant had been watching the news from The United Nations before we left and so had insisted that I pack for very cold weather. The other two tourists with me had strangely come equipped for the beach.

My glamorous sister and I were famous in the family for snoring very loudly and my niece had brought along a spray to stop us in our tracks and insisted on spraying her mother's throat. I politely desisted when she came towards me and I kept my teeth clamped together in a state of bruxism as I talked, just in case she made a rush at me.

My sister Gillian fell asleep within seconds but Claire said, "I really don't feel very well, in fact I am freezing" and so I swaddled her in cardigans, socks, a scarf and a jaunty woolly hat.

She sat propped up on pillows looking out of the floor length windows on to Times Square. When I was satisfied she was comfortable I tried to get into the other bed where my sister was

THE LOTUS GENERATION

sprawled out. I felt like an eight year old as I pushed and shoved her prone, sibling form. I eventually managed to sit propped up on the pillows and join Claire in looking out of the window.

Neither of us slept a wink that night. We just chatted about life in a desultory manner and the only excitement came about three am. My sister who had been snoring like a hippopotamus all night sat up in her sleep and thumped me very hard on the shoulder. "Stop snoring" she said in her best headmistress voice, "You are keeping me awake". She lay back down again and went back to sleep. Claire and I were still laughing at breakfast next morning.

I had been listening to the news and Broadway was on strike for the days that we were in town. The more I tried to explain this to my sister the more she insisted on standing in the queue. We queued in -10 degree cold until the men behind the counter told her that Broadway was on strike. "Gosh," she said, "fancy that". I restrained my urge to strangle her!

Gillian and Claire were in summer clothes and everyone was staring at us because we looked so out of place. I suggested that a trip to Macys or Bloomingdales was in order. We had a lovely shopping day and we bought a stylish coat each. I bought a navy raincoat for a woman about town, Claire bought a black trench coat for work and Gillian bought a long grey woollen coat with a faux fur collar.

As we set off the next day we felt very smart indeed. Gillian decided she wanted to go on an open top bus and so we made for the regular stop. Mother and daughter sat on the front seat on the left of the top of the bus and I sat on the right side. As the bus set off I realised that my feet were on the biggest block of ice I had ever seen, when I looked around to change seats I realised the bus was full of tourists. I spent the most uncomfortable two hours of my life with a rictus of a smile frozen on my face and a very cold derriere.

The trip was fun and we laughed a lot and saw most of the sites but I was glad to be back at home. I did however tuck a dollar in the back of my purse to remind me that I was going to go back sometime!

CHAPTER 22
The Fox In The Snow Storm

A fox is a wolf who sends flowers
Ruth Brown

Miranda was going back to work and I was going to look after my granddaughter Ellie. I knew in my heart that my daughter did not want to leave her daughter for three days a week. The decision had to be hers and her husband Alistair's and I said I would support them whatever they decided.

There was snow which was a foot deep the morning Miranda arrived to leave Ellie for the first time. My darling daughter looked dreadful and burst into tears. She lay down on the sofa and I rang her office to say she would not be in that day.

I covered her up and once I knew she was peacefully asleep I took Ellie into the kitchen. We stood at the French windows and gazed at the falling snow as I kissed the top of her perfect downy head. The pristine, powdery flakes brushed the window and Ellie traced them with her finger in wonder.

A magical wonderland stretched out before us. The sky had that surreal quality of an imminent snowfall. The sounds everywhere were muffled by the deep blanket of snow. The woodland at the bottom of the garden was almost unrecognisable except in outline.

Then from the midst of the trees in this silent, white world came the biggest red fox that I had ever seen. He was perfect in every way as he made his agile way down the garden path. His footprints left elegant impressions on the silent blanket of deep snow.

As I clasped my tiny granddaughter to my chest we both held our breath as the fox stopped and sniffed the air around him.

Satisfied that he was safe he continued to tip toe forwards until he reached the leaded French windows.

We watched him and he watched us for a long time. The snowflakes landed on his ochre coat before dissolving into a spider's web of moisture before our very eyes. The fox was majestic in every way and the kitchen light reflecting in his eyes made it seem as though he was smiling at us.

Finally he lifted his august head and sniffed the air and was gone with the gust of wind that blew across the garden.

Ellie smiled the kind of smile that squeezes your heart. I hugged her and smiled back and the fragrant coffee aroma reminded me why I had come into the kitchen in the first place.

My daughter decided to stay a few days until she was ready to venture back to work. We had a lovely time and she enjoyed being taken care of for a few days. We had bought a lovely new king size sleigh bed for the guest room and Grant had put it together a few weeks ago.

One morning I went upstairs to ask her what she would like for her breakfast. I sat on the side of the bed with Ellie on my lap and we were chatting happily away about the snowy weather, when suddenly we were all flung up in the air.

All three of us screamed as we crashed back down together and Miranda and I bumped heads. As we lay huddled breathless together on the floor we realised that the beautiful king size sleigh bed had collapsed. Once we had checked that Ellie was absolutely fine, Miranda struggled out of the bedclothes and got on to her feet.

"I guess that's my signal to go back to work" she said trying to control her mirth.

I will not report the conversation I had with Grant about his skills as a king size sleigh bed engineer.

CHAPTER 23
Looking After A Little Person

Grandchildren give us a chance to do things better because they bring out the best in us.

Anon.

A grandchild is a precious gift and the wonder of it is that you don't have to make any decisions. Their behaviour, education and everything else is up to somebody else.

All you get is the good times and the unfailing magic. We had so much fun in those two years before her little brother was born and Miranda decided to be a stay at home mum for a while.

THE LOTUS GENERATION

Ellie and I got into a perfect routine. Her mum dropped her off at eight am and for some reason she needed a little snooze that lasted exactly eighteen minutes before we did anything else.

When I offered her breakfast, porridge or Weetabix she would smile politely and eat five mouthfuls. If you offered her a sixth she would shake her head whilst clamping her gums firmly shut. Nothing you could do would persuade that child to have more than five mouthfuls of anything.

Miranda had an old flatmate, Zara from University, who was getting married and going to live in Australia. Zara rang me one afternoon and asked me to meet her in London to help her choose a wedding dress. She was having a winter wedding in England and less than a month later, a summer wedding in Australia.

I arranged to meet her in Kensington the next week. When I arrived at the appointed spot there was Zara and my daughter Miranda who was not being left out for anything.

We sailed in and out of all the wedding departments. We had such a fun time as she tried first one dress and then another but nothing was suitable. We were just beginning to show signs of total exhaustion when Zara had a brainwave. She decided she would have two different dresses for her two different weddings.

This made our commission much easier and we struck gold in the first emporium that we had the temerity to venture back inside.

The elegant assistant raised her eyebrows as she saw our party walking back towards her. When Zara mentioned a winter wedding she smiled and then first her head and then her whole black clad body disappeared into the racks of dresses. All we could see was the outline of her rather large quivering derriere.

"Ah, ha!" She shouted and out came the perfect outfit. A beautiful ballerina length dress and matching cape with a fur hood! Another assistant ran up to us with a pair of white boots and from nowhere came another assistant with a pearl coronet. Zara looked just like Grace Kelly, a perfect princess for her Australian groom.

A few weeks later I asked Miranda what she was going to buy them as a wedding present. "Well." she said "I was going to talk to you about that".

THE LOTUS GENERATION

"What", I said tentatively, knowing from past experience that this was going to involve me in some kind of lengthy carry on.

"I have agreed to make the wedding cake" she stated quietly. I did not speak but just looked at her through narrowing eyes.

"Zara wants a princess castle with turrets" she said to nobody in particular looking all around her.

My lips were now pursed to match my slit like eyes because I knew what was coming.

"I thought you would make it" she said quietly to the floor. I stood for a few moments and thought about the situation. I really, really did not want to make this cake.

I heard my voice say brightly "Ok then but we must decorate it at your house as it will make such a mess here."

"We can't" she said. "Can't what?" I replied.

"We can't make the cake at my house as poor Django is allergic to icing sugar. It makes him sneeze really badly" she said lamely.

Poor Django is a white, thirteen year old Birmin cat.

So began three months of baking, slicing, icing and moulding. Every kitchen surface was covered in a faint dust of icing sugar. You could taste it in the air and even the most savoury of dishes, like beef Bourgogne, seemed vaguely cloying on the palate.

I tried every way I could to make those turrets. I rolled icing, I tried modelling clay but nothing worked. Eventually I unwrapped four large rolls of industrial strength aluminium foil.

My mother had saved every piece of string, paper and ribbon she ever had. I felt so guilty throwing away armfuls of scrunched foil, but I felt it was all in a good cause. The day came that the cake was finished I was so delighted as it stood resplendent in all its glory perched on the kitchen table.

Miranda arrived back from work and looked at the majestic wedding cake. She turned it this way and that and examined every profile. I definitely heard a faint "mmm" escape her lips. I could feel my ears prickling and my hands getting very hot.

She picked up Ellie and put her arms round her middle so she that was facing forwards. "Well we think it's perfect, don't we darling?" and she smiled lovingly at her seven month old daughter. Her baby smiled back at her and then gave the turreted monstrosity a

THE LOTUS GENERATION

very sound kick with both feet. Then she let out the cutest giggle that I had ever heard in all my life.

There was a moment's silence as we surveyed the scene of devastation. Shock at the collapsed cake and delight at the giggle meant that we both burst out laughing.

Through my tears of laughter I said to Miranda "I wish your father had been here to see this".

"So do I" she said "but it really sounds like he is no longer with us."

She laughed and said "He has only popped to Waitrose for a bottle of wine".

When I worked out what it had cost me I realised that I could have bought Zara the most expensive cake in the local French patisserie and still had plenty of change.

I spent that weekend sticking everything back together and am pleased to report that Zara loved her cake.

At least that is what she said on her thank you note!

Chapter 24
Pearls And A Bracing Walk

A woman needs ropes and ropes of pearls.
Coco Chanel

Ellie and I walked for miles every single day. She loved anything pink and girly, so we went out dressed in our finery with pearls round our necks and princess stickers on every available surface.

Occasionally she insisted on wearing her actual shiny, pink princess dress for the whole day. I was required to wear a wedding hat with a big purple feather to match it if we went walking. I did get some funny looks in the very proper Home Counties in those halcyon days.

It was the hottest summer on record and reached 38.5 degrees. We spent those hot days under the shade of the apple trees in the side garden where it was cool and breezy.

THE LOTUS GENERATION

Ellie loved to read and we spent lots of time at the library. We swam and made cakes and every minute of every day was just perfect. We bought the piano from the lady next door and Ellie would bang out a tune and we would both sing along. For some reason she also loved Girls Aloud and The Black Eyed Peas and I am sure the neighbours gave us funny looks as they heard their albums blasting out through the open windows.

Ellie loved to climb, from about nine months she could go straight up the built in bookcase as though it was the north face of the Eiger. She gave her poor mother heart failure one afternoon. Miranda put her in her cot for an afternoon nap and went outside to hang the laundry out. Two minutes later she heard her shouting. When she went to look Ellie was at the top of the stairs. Every time you put her in her cot she did a perfect Fosbury Flop over the side. They bought her a bed that weekend and she had not even had her first birthday.

I came home from grocery shopping one day and put Ellie on the sofa in front of the television in the kitchen. As I handed her some juice I said, "Granny will be two seconds; I am just going to get the groceries from the hall where I left them"

As I walked back into the kitchen struggling with a twelve pack of loo rolls and some breakfast cereals there she stood on the kitchen table. She stared at me for a moment, shrugged her shoulders and then said "It's not dangerous" I vowed then I really would not take my eyes off her even for two seconds!

One day Miranda got home from work and announced with delight that she thought she was pregnant again. We were so thrilled but I knew my days looking after my granddaughter alone were numbered, as my daughter would be staying home this time with two children to look after.

I went to make a cup of tea and left Miranda sitting on the little French Louis XVI chair at the bottom of the stairs removing her boots. Ellie was standing next to her leaning against the antique French chest of drawers that matched the chair.

I looked back as I went into the kitchen thinking what a perfect picture they made.

I suddenly heard a really loud yell and went running back into the hall from the kitchen.

THE LOTUS GENERATION

My newly pregnant daughter was sitting clutching the side of her head staring at her precious fifteen month old daughter. Miranda had been bending forward as she removed her left boot from her foot. Ellie was standing in front of her holding the large antique clothes brush that was kept in the chest of drawers.

Ellie was the sweetest, gentlest little girl, but that day she had taken it upon herself to remove the clothes brush from the drawer and whack her mother smartly about the side of her head.

Tears ran down my daughters face "Ow, ow, ow" she stammered. Then she started to laugh "The little madam must have heard me say I was having another baby!"

Miranda was delighted that she was having a baby boy, but she worked right up until the end of her pregnancy. My heart nearly stopped every morning as she squeezed her ever expanding girth behind the wheel of a car. I thought to myself "How things have changed in a generation".

When I was pregnant you were required to wear a smock from about four months to hide your tiny bump, now women just wear what they wear and if the bump showed it does not matter.

When I was pregnant you had to stop work at 28 weeks and stare out of the window, in the fashion of a Bronte sister but now women worked until the day they gave birth.

That spring went lazily by and we all looked forward to the new baby's arrival. Miranda was in a London hospital and we took our little granddaughter in to meet Felix, her new brother. My daughter rang in the middle of the night and I panicked and thought something was wrong with her or the baby.

It took me a while to calm down so I could understand what she was saying. Her husband who was in an adjoining room had left the bath running and fallen asleep and the room below had to be evacuated.

I spent lots of time with my new grandson but slowly my daughter's life changed to that of a stay at home mum and she had new interests. Her life changed and so did mine as I had lots of free time again.

I felt sort of sad and just a little redundant, as if my reason for being had been taken away from me.

I woke up one morning and said to myself quite firmly "You need to get off your bottom and start concentrating on your career, my girl."

CHAPTER 25
We Are Off To Yorkshire For A Wedding

Marriage is like a violin: when the sweet music is over the strings are still attached.

Anon.

Ten days after my new grandson, Felix, was born my niece Claire was married three hundred miles from where we lived. My daughter was determined to attend this wedding as she and Claire had always been very close.

Claire was about to marry her wonderful policeman, Robert, and the wedding was to be held in a beautiful old Abbey which was surrounded by ruins. We all stayed at an elegant hotel nearby but Miranda had decided to drive up that day.

Eventually we were all in the Abbey waiting for the bride when my daughter, her husband and her two children came rushing up the aisle and settled in their seats.

Two minutes later the beautiful bride walked down the aisle, she had been sitting in the bridal car, with her dad Malcolm, outside the Abbey and refused to get married until her cousin was in her place!

The service was wonderful but when the new bride and groom knelt down a voice rang out round the Abbey. My granddaughter Ellie, just two at the time spoke up loudly with a useful piece of advice. "Oh Claire, please get up off your knees, you will ruin your beautiful princess dress". A ripple of laughter went round the congregation and we all relaxed and really enjoyed what was a very moving service.

The reception was excellent and when the dancing began at nine pm I said to Grant "Let's take the children up to their room and let our daughter have an hour with all the cousins". I woke up at two am with my daughter shaking me awake. "Thanks, Mum I will take over from here." She had had a lovely time dancing at the party and I thought how radiant she looked.

THE LOTUS GENERATION

A political event that saddened me this year was the 2004 New Higher Education Bill introducing variable repayable top up fees of up to £ 3000 a year. The 1998 introduction of £1000 fees for students had meant the end of free education in Great Britain. Free education for all had been one of the foundations of our British society. I knew that other countries paid for their further education as I had experience of this with family in Canada and America.

I really hoped that this amount would not put teenagers off the important and productive experience of a university education.

In December that year the Tsunami hit Indonesia and Thailand and lots of lives were lost. It was a shocking event and made people realise just how powerless human beings are against the might of nature.

I also watched the first of the many hundreds of *Pepper Pig* programmes that I was destined to see in my lifetime. I became familiar with the whole family including George who seemed to be every small child's favourite younger brother.

I also heard the music of the Scissor Sisters, everywhere I went and funnily enough I grew to think they were absolutely wonderful!

Another of the programmes that my late mother stayed up past nine pm for was *Question Time* with David Dimbleby. The television programme celebrated its 25 years anniversary on air this year.

However we all preferred the radio version of *Any Questions* that had been running for many years and was chaired by his younger brother Jonathan Dimbleby.

Our very favourite Radio programme was, without question, *Letter from America* by Alistair Cooke. The sound of his mellifluous voice was balm to the soul and stopped you in your tracks whatever task you were engrossed in.

Alistair Cook was ninety five years old when he finally retired from presenting his Radio Four Friday night programme. It had been running since March 1946 and he had presented 2,869 episodes. His 15 minute vignettes of observation and anecdote gave an Americanophile like me more interesting information about what was going on over the pond, than all the articles I read in the newspapers.

Our third radio favourite was *Gardeners Question Time*.

Grant and I had enjoyed being in the audience of Question Time when it was in London and Gardeners Question Time when it came to a village near us in the Lakes.

When Claire's wedding photographs arrived I could not believe my eyes. I had bought the large chiffon pale green hat to match my suit in a hurry and not tried it on my head since. In every single photo the hat had slid down over my face and I was completely invisible. I went straight up to my wardrobe, stuffed the offending hat into a Waitrose carrier bag and dropped it off at the charity shop.

CHAPTER 26
My Slip On The Disney Trip

Our greatest glory is not in never falling, but rising every time we fall.
Confucius

My intentions to be industrious were well meant but people kept inviting me on exciting adventures. Miranda and her husband Alistair wanted us to go to Disneyland Paris with them and their children .We stayed in a rather swish hotel near all the amenities and that was useful, because it rained "that Lake District misty rain that really wets you through" for the whole time we were there.

One morning we set off all wearing the obligatory yellow rain macs that had huge hoods and skimmed the floor. As we walked across a tiled piazza I noticed how our family group had spread out.

Grant and Miranda walked in front chatting away, I was somewhat behind, parading Felix in his pushchair and Alistair was a long way behind with Ellie on his shoulders. As I glanced around I could not miss my son-in-law as he is 6'4" and had a child on his shoulders. They both looked like a very large yellow bear from a distance, if I squinted carefully.

I had on an exquisite pair of holiday shoes. I had had them for years and they were carefully designed out of shapes of leather red apples, suede oranges and patent yellow bananas. They had been very expensive and got lots of admiring glances and I really loved them. The only problem was that they were very slippery on marble tiles.

THE LOTUS GENERATION

As I carefully stepped one foot after the other disaster struck just outside the sweet shop. Going, going, gone, too late I was flat on my back with a sleeping six month old blonde cherub hanging upside down on top of me.

I surveyed the shops from my prone position and I thought, "Thank goodness I am in this yellow all in one so that nobody can recognise me." Eventually my terribly proper son-in-law Alistair strolled up and said "Oh goodness me, mother-in-law what are you doing down there? Do you need a hand to get up?"

As I looked up from the floor at my granddaughter who was seven feet in the air I said "Please tell your daddy that Felix and I are fine lying here on the floor in the rain and we will wait for a member of the Disney staff to rescue us, thank you!"

He gave a loud snort, the pram was upright and I was on my feet and we were on our way all in a few seconds. He managed to do all that with a child still balancing on his shoulders. All those years of rowing and marathon running were not wasted.

I was still holding the balloons of Mickey and Minnie Mouse that I had bought for the children. We tied the strings to the back of a chair whilst we went to the rodeo show plus cowboy meal in the pouring rain.

There was such a lot of western style, heeing and hawing going on as the cowboys ran round the sawdust ring. The lovely grey and piebald horses seemed to be having a great time but the both the Cowboys and Indians both seemed a little out of breath in my opinion.

They were good at thigh slapping and shouting loudly and I hoped they would turn the volume down in the second half. We were all high up in the auditorium and sitting closely together. Miranda had her expensive brown leather handbag on her lap and her elbow firmly lodged in my solar plexus.

The children were both fast asleep and lay uncomfortably across their father's knees. The cowgirls brought the food round and chilli appeared to be the order of the evening. I suddenly had a very hot turn and my daughter signalled to me over the din. She scrabbled about in the bottom of her bag for a fluff covered antihistamine that looked as though it had been in there for a long time.

I did as I was silently bidden and obediently swallowed it with some trepidation along with the offered can of warm fizzy pop. I did not have the heart to tell her it was my advancing age that was causing the hot flush not an allergic reaction to the chilli peppers.

When we got back to the room, Ellie who was just a little way in front of us with her mummy lay sobbing on the floor. We could not get any sense out of her she just kept saying "Poor Minnie, oh poor Minnie". Then we realised that Minnie and Mickey had floated to the top of a twelve foot high ceiling. Some practical joker member of staff had come into the room to turn down the beds and had cut the string attaching them to the chair.

We thought about reporting them but it seemed petty. However Minnie had to be rescued before Ellie would contemplate sleep. Grant eventually stood on his rower son-in-law shoulders and delivered them back to earth without breaking his own neck. It was however touch and go there for a few minutes.

I think that week's weather made me the wettest I have ever been in all my life and I nursed a very sore posterior which stopped me going on any of the rides. Thank goodness!

Chapter 27
My Little Sister's Gone To Spain

Through travel I became aware of the outside world; it was through travel that I found my own way into becoming part of it.

Eudora Welty.

My sister Gillian had been a headmistress and decided to retire in her late forties. Her husband Malcolm had had a lifelong dream to live abroad and they had decided to take the plunge. His sister now lived in a scenic part of Spain and that is where they were headed.

My sister and our husbands had all been friends since childhood as we attended the same school and so had spent many convivial evenings discussing a day dream to open a hotel in France.

Gillian spoke perfect French and so she would be front of house. Malcolm with his ebullient personality and knowledge of fine wines was going to run the bar. Grant is an excellent cook so he fancied himself as the chef and we all agreed with his plan.

That just left me as jack-of-all-trades. One evening as the lengthy discussion drew to a wine fuelled, desultory conclusion I decided to put in my two-penny worth. "I guess that just leaves me with the housekeeper's job then" I said a little petulantly, even to my ears. They all turned to face me and stared. Eventually my sister conceded "Well I can help you with the cleaning".

I closed my eyes and began to shake with mirth. I had a mental image of my immaculately turned out sister in full makeup holding a feather duster and I was on my knees scrubbing away dressed like Julie Walter's Mrs Overall with a scarf wrapped round my head. Whenever that particular plan raised its head again I tried to change the subject as it was a non-starter as far as I was concerned.

When I heard they were going to live in Spain I was delighted and could not wait to visit them.

They were living in the North of England at the time and they called in to see us on their way to the ferry. They had sold their lovely car and bought what could only be described as a red Postman Pat's van. I knew my sister would be sad leaving her home and I was rather worried about her. As they pulled up on the drive I noticed a rather pinched expression on Gillian's face. I made her a stiff drink and sat her down "How did it go?" I empathised.

"Well she said, moving out was alright but by the time we finished packing the little van was rather full. I did not want to be seen by my pupils in this ridiculous contraption so I slid down on the floor until we had left the neighbourhood".

I really wanted to laugh at the thought of my elegant sister on the floor of the car but something about the look on her face stopped me in my tracks.

CHAPTER 28
I Really Like This Place

Loving life is easy when you are abroad. Where no-one knows you and you hold your life in your hands alone, you are more a master of yourself than at any other time.

Hannah Arendt.

We waited a couple of weeks then decided to follow them. I was a little concerned about my sister and wanted to be sure she was alright. We took a flight to Alicante airport and then hired a car to drive north. Where they had chosen to live was between Valencia and Alicante but flights to Alicante were much more frequent.

As we left Alicante we drove the coast road north. The sun was beginning to set and the shimmering reflection across the sea matched anything I had ever seen anywhere in the world. I relaxed back into my seat and began to breathe.

The home they had chosen was right in the centre of the town but had a view of the mountains through the orange groves on one side and a view of the crystal sea from the other window. She was waiting at the door to greet me, tanned and relaxed she looked ten years younger than she had weeks before.

Malcolm shepherded us in and offered us a celebratory glass of Cava. The table was set with tapas in every colour, sitting proudly in the traditional Spanish earthen ware dishes. Red peppers, fat green olives, tiny pink prawns and yellow Manchigo cheese set on a bright blue checked cloth. They showed us round and then we headed out to enjoy the town.

They had booked us into a fish restaurant on the quayside and to get there we had to walk down the main street. It was Saturday evening and the Spanish people were out on all their finery. The Passeo, which is an evening, easy stroll taken by everyone from the smallest baby to the oldest resident. The Spaniards dress up for this and it is a chance to meet up with friends and family

There seemed to be a party atmosphere that night that made you feel glad to be alive. We did not eat until ten pm which seemed very late, but I was to learn later that Spanish afternoons go on well into the evening.

The restaurant served us monk fish wrapped in Serrano ham with a huge salad. Later they brought us Crèma Catalane and small glasses of fiery brandy. Nobody rushed and everybody smiled and wished you well.

We headed out of the restaurant for the short walk to the jazz club where we were to relax for the rest of the evening. A lady stopped us and asked, "Que hora es?" My brother-in-law looked at his watch and I was amazed by his answer "Son las dos y cinco."

It was after two am but I really did not care, which was not like me at all….

We danced the night away to a Dutch jazz band playing on the water front. The night was warm and the stars were bright and I felt as though I had not a care in the world .We walked slowly home arm in arm singing our version of the wonderful songs we had heard. I fell slowly back on to the bed and the room had a definite suggestion of a shimmery movement. It's the heat affecting me I thought.

As I was just drifting off I am sure I heard a distant voice whispered in my mind. "I think you will find it is the sherry, wine and brandy that you consumed in that order!"

The next morning the bright sunlight assaulted my retinas long before I was ready to be awakened. I must have made an "Aargh" sound so my kind husband got up and pressed the button to close the blackout blind. He then made another sound entirely as he stubbed his toe on the bedframe as he stumbled about in the dark.

I waited until he was comfortably ensconced back in bed and then croaked "I really need a drink of water". He sighed a very voluble sigh and lifted his weary body up on one elbow. I heard him scrabble about on the bedside table. "Here is a glass of water, dear" he announced into the dark in a faintly exasperated tone.

I reached across to take the proffered receptacle in the dark. He let go before I had chance to complete my grip. The only good about the next two frantic minutes was that the water had had chance to warm up in the night before it drenched every single bit of us.

We were both saturated and I was sharply tasked with finding the light switch. Ten minutes later, after eating tomato tostas, drinking strong cortados and apologising to our hosts, we were whizzing up and down the azure blue swimming pool.

I stepped out of the pool as Gillian and I were going shopping and as I wound a towel around my hair I looked up. The view was breathtaking and it was in that moment that my love affair with Spain began.

CHAPTER 29
Mrs. Fanshaw Is In The Changing Room

Happiness is the sublime moment when you get out of your corsets at night.
Joyce Grenfell

The shopping trip started well. I love shoes and was hoping to buy a pair whilst I was there. The trouble was that Spanish women have small feet and I have rather large ones. Gillian bought two pairs and I left the shop feeling like Cinderella must have felt on her very worst day.

We decided to look for evening dresses as we had been invited by a friendly neighbour to a Masonic formal dance the next evening. The clothes were elegant and beautifully made and so we went in first one shop and then another searching through the gorgeous racks of clothes. We both discovered dresses in one shop that we liked and with our arms laden we headed for the tiny private changing room.

My sister is built like me, just a much thinner version. Spanish clothes are made for slender women with small chests and we are both blessed with Grandmother Alexandra's ample embonpoint. We stood facing each other in the changing room like characters in a Joyce Grenfell monologue. I felt like portly Mrs Fanshaw about to dance "Stately as a Galleon" as we stood bust to bust.

Gillian made the first move by putting the fitted bodice of the evening dress over her head and then tried to pull it back off again as she realised it would not go past her ample bust. She immediately began to hyperventilate as she realised her arms were stuck in the air. "Help me, help" me was the muffled cry from inside the thick material. I started to laugh uncontrollably.

"You mean horrible sister, you know I have claustrophobia." I started to laugh even more until the sharp kick she administered to my

THE LOTUS GENERATION

shin changed my cheery mood. "OK what do you want me to do,?" I said as I peered down the top to see a very red face and dishevelled hair.

"Please pull it off you silly woman, you are so useless!," she cried. Well I pulled this way and that and her body on its four inch heels staggered first this way and that. I had started laughing again as I was reminded of the fights to the death we used to have as small children.

In the end I said "I am sorry I will have to calm down" and I sat down on the rickety bench. She flopped down beside me. "I really am cross with you" she said. Well I think that was what she said as her head was still inside an inside out evening dress and her arms were in the air like she was being robbed at gunpoint.

"Look here" I said as I put my glasses on and began to examine the zip. A few tugs here and a quick yank there and in one bound she was free. I put the dress back on the hanger and nobody would have known the difference.

We said our goodbyes to the bemused girl in the shop and staggered next door for a cold drink. I had a gin and tonic and she had a vodka and diet coke and we put the world to rights as the sun went down over the sea.

I very rarely drink but I was enjoying the ice cold liquid with the bobbing lemon slices and as they kept bringing them to me I kept drinking them.

Two hours later as we decided to go back to meet the boys I discovered that I could not walk in a straight line and after a small heated discussion a taxi had to be summoned.

We had wonderful fun that week. We drove up in the mountains, picked oranges off the trees and swam in the sea. The brisk afternoon Lavante wind that disturbed all our possessions on the beach soon gave way to a gentle zephyr.

It seems a magical place to be as the people were delightful, the cost of living inexpensive and the pound to the euro exchange rate really worked in our favour. A delicious meal in a restaurant, a Menu del Dias, was only a few Euros so cooking an evening meal was not mandatory!

THE LOTUS GENERATION

Gillian and Malcolm seemed to have made so many friends in the weeks that they were there that they were out every night. We dined in a Brazilian restaurant and listened to three university lecturers from Barcelona playing their exquisite guitar music from flamenco to the Beatles. We sang our hearts out to the songs we knew and danced to the ones we didn't.

In fact my husband actually ended up dancing on the table. He was invited up there by the patron as he was the tallest man in the room. He had been instructed to mend the ceiling fan and then overcome with being the centre of attention; he gave us a little two step shuffle before dismounting with a flourish.

The result of that foolhardy carry on meant that he put his back out. He moaned and groaned for the next two hours and I studiously ignored his garbled entreaties.

It was that night, noticing a bowl of limes on the bar that I remembered a long forgotten drink, Gimlet, half vodka and half fresh lime juice served over ice.

Tasting the first proffered glass I decided I agreed with Raymond Chandler in the 1953 film *The Long Goodbye*. "A real gimlet is half gin and half Roses lime juice....nothing else."

We joined a wedding party dancing on the beach and stayed until dawn. Grant and I especially the classical concerts in the churches played into the night. The fascinating thing for me was their ladies and their fans. They waved them back and forth in unison creating a cooling draught on a hot summer's day. Spanish churches are stunningly ornate and decorative and your eyes are drawn this way and that as you listen to the haunting music.

I could have stayed there forever but too soon it was time to go home. They drove us to the airport and as we waved a tearful goodbye we all agreed we had not had so much fun since we were teenagers.

CHAPTER 30
The South American Trip

All the resources we need are in our mind.
Theodor Roosevelt

I closed my eyes for just a moment as the gentle, soothing rhythm of the train lulled me into the arms of Morpheus. I could feel the inside of my husband's warm wrist against mine through the crisp cotton of his blue Oxford shirt. Within seconds, it seemed, I was unwillingly dragged back into wakefulness by a fierce, hot shot of adrenalin pumping all through my body. The first thought to enter my brain was "I know I must have been asleep because I have that slight metallic taste on my tongue."

It was during the next burst of reality, when I had really no idea where I was, an esoteric farrago so tumultuous, so loud, crashed and banged its way into my foggy brain.

The powerful noise was in fact The EL Tamborito band, The Little Drum or Tamborito that is the music and dance of Panamanian Folklore. I forced my eyes open and stretched my neck out to check out its restricted movement. First this way and that before realising that the percussion section, and particularly the man with the cymbals, was warming up just behind my head. Then, out of the mist I finally remembered where we were.

We were on a train journey between Puerto Colon, near the Caribbean entrance to the Panama Canal, and Panama City on the Pacific Coast. The Panama Canal Railway is one of the great unknown train rides of the world. The railroad follows a picturesque path across the Isthmus of Panama. The carriage was so evocative of the nineteenth century but comfortable with a cool breeze playing across the warm air.

Our journey on the scenic railway line flanked the Panama Canal. The train swished through lush rainforests, cruised alongside the Canal's locks, through the historic Gaillard Cut and passed over the slender causeways in the Gatun Lake.

The band and dancers were dressed in the national costume of Panama. The women's dresses are called Polleras and are handmade and the adult girls dress should last them for life. They are designed in beautiful colours of pink and blue with animals and flowers on a white background. The dresses normally take a year to make and can cost hundreds or even thousands of dollars.

The gold and pearl Mosquetas and Temblques head dresses are generally passed down as heirlooms through the generations. Men wear the traditional Montuno outfits with traditional hats that recall life in the country side.

The dancers played and sang their way up and down the corridor of the luxury train. They handed out sweetmeats and local drinks and told stories of their ancestors and their quest for wealth during the California Gold Rush. The trip took about two hours which gave us lots of time to explore Panama City.

I was thoroughly enjoying the last minute cruise break that I had booked for our wedding anniversary. I knew that if I had given Grant a choice he would have wrinkled his nose before he said "OK" so I decided to spring it on him. So far, so good and the cabin with its balcony had found favour with him.

We were able to sit out in the late afternoon gazing at the startling blue of the Caribbean Sea whilst sipping a martini. We were also enjoying a late brandy and coffee whist counting the lustrous stars in the inky midnight sky.

The plane journey to Barbados had been without incident and we had only just disembarked when we were on our way to the cruise ship.

We were having some garden renovations done at home and it was not going to plan. A renegade bamboo plant had taken four large men, five days to dig out as it had made its way under the kitchen. We were glad to be away from home for a couple of weeks.

The cabin on the cruise ship was delightful and having your luggage appear without effort got my vote. We were to be away for eighteen days and as well as Panama were going to visit Costa Rica, Mexico, Aruba, Dominican Republic Mexico and the Cayman Islands.

One of our sons had spent some time in the Dominican Republic as he was friends with a boy from school whose father was the Governor there. We also had friends Lily and Boris that lived in the Cayman Islands, who we were hoping to catch up with.

THE LOTUS GENERATION

Lily and Boris were always such fun. They had a ranch in Texas where they kept a yellow Rolls Royce as well as a house in Switzerland where we had been their guests. We looked forward to being with them but first of all we had lots of exciting places to visit.

CHAPTER 31
The Winding Jungle Path

A brave heart and a courteous tongue: They shall carry thee far through the jungle, manling.

Rudyard Kipling

I have an image in my mind so profound that I can close my eyes and summon up that a perfect place in a heartbeat. I have an amazing work of art that will take me to that place even quicker.

I can see a dark green background of trees with bright blue skies peeping out between the leaves. Bright orange parrots with proud yellow chests sit on the branches of the trees and toucans in their entire azure finery peep round tumbling corners. There are swathes of purple butterflies and yellow tree climbing frogs. There is a slumbering sloth hanging upside down and a friendly looking leopard oversees his patch of the jungle.

When my eyes are closed I am back in Costa Rica. This beautiful country is located on the Isthmus that separates North and South America. Costa Rica is a natural habitat for the many types of flora and fauna that are found in both of those continents. The micro climate of the mountains, the rivers and forests allow all life to flourish. The forest teems with life and the lush vegetation is home to many different species of plants, some with heady scents.

The birds and butterflies with colours of blue, red, yellow and purple flash by and are gone. The frequent rain showers wash everything clean and then the sun is out again.

The piece of art I brought home with me? My perfect umbrella of course, sitting every day in its stand by the front door it lifts my spirits on the rainiest of occasions.

I brought it from an old lady in a little shack and it gives me a frisson of pleasure every single day. No matter which queue I am

THE LOTUS GENERATION

standing in, the grey skies are gone in a moment and I am back with the scents and sounds of the jungle.

Costa Rica is an amazing country with a very stable economy that depends on tourism and agriculture. It also is very forward thinking with a highly educated population and exports a lot of electronics.

We managed a trip through the forest and the most adventurous of the party went up high on a wire for a different perspective.

We were also offered a trip to a banana plantation. Frankly when you have seen one of these you have seen them all, I had not got the heart to say no and a feeling of pathos meant I spent the time wandering around the banana shop spending my money. I have a little Spanish and so I was able to chat to some of the women and children and I enjoyed my afternoon.

Being on a cruise ship is a strange experience. The thought that you can eat what you like when you like is a little unnerving. A friend of mine had warned "If you go on a cruise ship be careful of catching farctate." She laughed at my puzzled face. "Was it a contagious disease?" I asked.

I laughed as well when I looked it up in the dictionary "The state of being stuffed with food by overeating!" After some discussion and to assuage the guilt we decided to march three times round the poop deck, three times a day. I am sure we looked a little crackers but our consumption of indigestion tablets was kept to a minimum.

The food was excellent whichever restaurant you went in. My favourite dish was the crab cakes that a young chef from Blackpool made us one night after we had been out dancing.

First thing every morning a deeply tanned chap of uncertain years stood dressed in his blue micro speedos and posed Mr Universe style against the rails outside the breakfast restaurant.

Diners rushed to grab the seats facing the other way. If you were unfortunate enough to have Mr Universe in your eye line you were obliged to eat your porridge with your eyes firmly closed.

One morning I went down for an early lunch as Grant was having a golf lesson and sat with a group of older ladies. Sparkly and gregarious to a woman they told me that when their husbands had died they had sold their homes and spent the proceeds on one long eternal cruise. They looked so happy and relaxed but what their children thought about this matter was not recorded.

I had always had a fancy to visit the Cayman Islands. Our friends had told us so much about it as they had owned a house on the Island for decades. We were meeting Lily and Boris for lunch on the harbour as we only had four hours before returning to the ship.

As we disembarked from the small boat that had brought us to the shore I took my first look around. Banks, jewellers and restaurants were the order of the day. As far as the eye could see very smart people were going about their business, which was either working in a bank, jewellers or restaurant?

I did not need a bank as everything just turned up miraculously on a cruise ship but I could certainly do with a drink and jewellers in that order. After a quick coffee we made our way through the doors of the first emporium that we could see. Counter after counter of the most exquisite jewellery was laid out to tempt the starry-eyed traveller.

After much looking and some touching I chose a tiny white gold heart shaped pendant, encrusted with rubies and diamonds. I just loved it and as I turned to kiss my husband in thanks a voice I knew boomed, "What's going on here then?"

It was our friend Boris who stood beaming in the doorway. Lily was just behind him and we were so delighted to see them. They took us for a delicious fish lunch and we just had time to look at the turtles in the harbour when we had to say goodbye.

We took so long saying our farewells that we had to jump on the last boat back to the cruise ship with promises to meet back up again in England when they got back from their holidays.

CHAPTER 32
A Cold Marguerita in Cancun, Anyone?

Summer drinking rules no 3. Margaritas count as your daily serving of fruit.
Anon.

Once I got used to being on a cruise ship I really began to love the pace of life. We had a long leisurely lie in bed with the sun shining through the open terrace doors and the breeze moving the bight, white sheer curtains. The sound of the ocean lapping against the hull of the ship almost masked the waiter's breakfast knock.

We had croissants, fresh fruit and coffee on the balcony staring out over an expanse of ocean so blue that there are no words to describe the colour, except Caribbean.

Most days after breakfast, I went to Pilates or for a beauty treatment before meeting Grant for a delicious lunch. The hardest question of the day was "which restaurant should we eat in?" Afternoons were spent sunbathing and reading before a snooze and a small aperitif in the cabin. We made lots of friends and enjoyed their company at dinner.

Shuffleboard Games on the deck sounded like something out of an Agatha Christie novel but once you got into the swing of things people were great fun. Some evenings were formal and people got dressed up in long dresses and evening jackets. Themed parties late in the night on deck and shows from Broadway all added to the feel of being in a time out of time.

We visited Mexico on one particular day at a private beach club at Cancun. The sun was hot and I sat for hours by the side of the water whilst a delightful waiter brought me the most delicious margaritas that I had ever tasted. I could see Grant sitting out on the walkway, with his legs dangling, staring pensively out into the water. Eventually I decided to walk across to see him.

As I struggled to my feet one of the waiters came to take my arm and escort me to my destination. He smilingly left me with my husband. I said, " How wonderfully polite of that young man to escort me to you." He laughed and said, " I am not sure about polite I think he just wondered if you would make it over here. How many margaritas have you had?" I tried to count them but gave it up as a bad job on such a sunny and blissful day. All that was left of them was the faint taste of salt as I brushed my tongue against my lips.

The cruise ended but the journey home was a little fraught. We had to wait for hours at Barbados Airport outside in the midday sun. This would have been boring except for the fact that various famous faces from the cricketing and show business world kept walking past. To be honest I really did not know who half of them were but it felt churlish not to join in with the frankly crackers game of celebratory cheering.

Eventually we got on the plane hot, bothered and cranky. Just as we thought we must be heading towards London the captain announced we were running out of fuel and would have to stop at Dublin to pick up some more.

Eventually we arrived two hours late and Miranda who was waiting for us was rather worried. We decided there and then that we would always get a taxi in future when arriving from a long hall flight.

We talked endlessly about cruise trips when we got home but the truth is that we have never, ever been on another one.

CHAPTER 33
Could You Just Get Me Some Apples Please?

You can count the apples from a tree but you cannot count the trees from one apple.

Old proverb

I awoke to the dulcet tones of John Humphries as I did every morning. We had always listened to Radio Four but just lately Grant had been tuning into Radio Five especially if he had been awake in the night. I turned over to realise he had left me a cup of tea as he had done every morning of our married life and I really appreciated the gesture.

The sunlight was streaming through the pale cream curtains and I decided to take the opportunity to have an early stroll around the garden. As I walked through the French windows I was surprised to see Grant out there pacing the garden with his tape measure.

Our pretty garden was series of different rooms. The bottom of the garden housed the shed and the herb and vegetable garden. On the left of the house were the apple and pear trees with the children's slide and swings arranged around them. Rambling roses scrambled through the trees and the scintillating scent at that side of the house always lingered in the air.

We had experienced a particular apple tree incident when the perfect red apples were at their finest. As with any fruit tree the sweetest and best fruit is always at the top and Grant was busy picking this fruit when his ladder overbalanced. I was further down the garden picking plums from the safety of Mother Earth when out of the corner of my eye I saw him overbalance.

Anyone who knows me will tell you I am not a runner and I have no idea what I intended to achieve that day as I sprinted across the lawn shouting "Don't worry love, I will catch you!"

All I can say in my defence is that it must have been a very primeval instinct.

Grant fell smartly out of the fifteen foot tree yelling all sorts of expletive deletives. Fortunately he had a very soft landing on his well upholstered wife. I had arrived seconds before he landed and had broken his fall with my body.

He lay with his body on top of mine bruised and winded but none the worse for his adventure. I was slightly more bruised and winded being a lady with a large embonpoint but thankfully still breathing.

Well actually we were struggling to breathe because we were laughing so much. First one neighbour and then another arrived to see what the commotion was and they ended up hysterical too because nobody could get us on our feet no matter how hard they tried.

Eventually it all calmed down and we went inside for a cup of tea that turned into a party. I smiled through it all until I was able to put arnica on my purpling bruises at midnight.

CHAPTER 34
There Is About To Be Some Remodelling

In the language of flowers the Jasmine flower symbolises sweetness, kindness, beauty and happiness.

Anon.

There was a huge wooden Heath Robinson affair that was attached to the house on the right side. Built by a previous occupant to house his large boat it now contained the stuff of family life bikes, scooters, dolls houses, scalectric sets and gardening equipment.

There was a particularly stubborn winter flowering jasmine plant that scrambled inside and out of Heath Robinson. I tried to cut it back but it meant risking life and limb so I gave it up as a bad job. One morning I was vacuuming the bedroom carpet and there it was a beautiful creamy pink jasmine plant that had made its way through concrete and then up through carpet for my delectation.

A large, sunny conservatory went across the back of the house and an arbour full of summer flowering plants geraniums, fuchsias and petunias showed their faces to the sun outside the kitchen door.

The rooms were divided by different plants but a particular one would have kept a family of pandas sated. It was of course the dreaded bamboo. There were still lots there even though the gardeners had been hard at it whilst we were away.

"This garden needs a full makeover, to be brought up to date for the modern world" my husband announced to nobody in particular

"Good luck with that" I thought and tried to slink back into the kitchen. As I walked back in I glanced at the kitchen clock as it was still only six thirty.

I poured two cups of coffee and handing one to Grant I announced my intention to go back to bed for an hour with the paper which had just been posted through the door.

I had just got back in bed when he came and sat down next to me. I sighed and tried hard to hide the expression on my face. Whatever he had in mind I would rather be reading the Guardian and so I was mightily relieved when he produced a notebook and pen out of his jeans pocket.

THE LOTUS GENERATION

"The whole house needs remodelling and I am going to spend this year doing It." he said.

"Perfect, thank you" was my reply. I loved this house and would enjoy the project.

Doors appeared where windows once had been. Fireplaces went out in pieces through the back door and brand new elegant ones came triumphantly in through the front.

Every visitor was requisitioned to bring something into the house with them. The postman was to be seen helping with the bags of plaster, the milkman helped with a large fireplace and a passing vicar helped lug the black marble work surfaces into the kitchen.

A definite feeling of camaraderie filled the air in those months. We decided to overlook it when our neighbours broke skip protocol. We had just a new skip delivered when Jim next door asked if he could put a few things in it, of course we agreed.

The next morning we got up to realise he had cheekily filled it completely during the night. Whilst I was ringing the company to come and collect it again, Grant ran out and put an empty paint tin on the top. "Ready to go now" he shouted resignedly.

Every wall was painted and some were even plastered to create arches where none had been. Cornices appeared at the top of every wall and the house began to look simply perfect. A new kitchen arrived and was expertly fitted and the last job left to do was to renovate a downstairs cloakroom. Grant decided to do that himself as we were just about beginning to run out of resources.

One winter's day I had popped to Sainsbury's and as luck would have it had met everyone I knew. I must have been gone for two hours when I turned my key in the front door. Grant was very quiet as he leaned on the breakfast bar and then I stopped chattering when I saw the colour of his face.

"Ok what's wrong" I said concerned. I had actually no need to ask as he undid the tea towel wrapped around his hand. His finger was in two pieces dangling by a thread. He had been trying to smash the sink with a hammer and as it fell he had caught it instinctively. His finger had come off worse than the sink.

We spent the night at the hospital and the wonderful young doctor with tremendous skill with a needle and thread saved the finger. His platinum wedding band did not live to tell the tale.

Next day I got the plumbers in to finish the job and before Christmas the house looked immaculate in all its glory. As I looked around I had a very strange thought from nowhere in particular. "Every time we finished a house we always move. We always move, every time without exception. I shook myself out of my reverie.

"Why would I ever leave here?," I thought, "I am really settled."

CHAPTER 35
Two Gay Pride Parades In One Day

I would rather regret the things I have done rather the things I haven't.
Lucille Ball

I had absolutely no intention of being in Toronto. I absolutely did not intend being in the middle of a Gay Pride parade whilst deciding where to go for lunch, but life has a funny way of changing your plans. I have one inviolate rule when travelling "If something cool appears to be happening then just roll with it .What is the worst that can happen?"

My other travelling mantra however is a little more prosaic. "Never stand when you can sit, never sit when you can lie and never, ever pass an available loo."

We had a longstanding invitation to visit Grant's cousin Susie in Santa Barbara, California. James our youngest son had stayed with them when he was living in Canada. Then we received an invite to my cousin Joshua's wedding in Vancouver, so we decided to combine both trips. Our son James had expressed his intention to go to the wedding as Joshua had been good to him on his gap year sojourn. He rang me one morning and said "Can you organise my flights as well, please Mum"

Within an hour I had booked flights to San Francisco, booked a car to take us from there to Santa Barbara and on to Las Vegas. Then at last a flight on to Vancouver and home again, all in fourteen days.

THE LOTUS GENERATION

I sent the details to James and Grant expecting copious thanks for my efficiency.

First one and then the other rang and said the same thing "You do know the flight to San Francisco you have booked stops in Toronto?"

Well no, I didn't but it made sense as we were travelling with a Canadian airline.

Then I remembered Sars or severe acute respiratory syndrome. Toronto had two outbreaks of the acute respiratory syndrome virus in the last couple of years and the last one had been quite recent. I thought about it and said "Everything will be OK; we are not there for long".

We landed in Toronto after an uneventful flight and piled on the bus to take us to change planes. We stood as it never takes long, does it? Three quarters of an hour later we were still driving round the airport as it was a very long way. We waited by the carousel looking for our cases but they never arrived. The airport began to get quieter and more silent. It was definitely touch and go whether we would make our onward flight.

Then James spied our cases, trapped at the top of a conveyor belt. "I can do this", he said with determination and started to climb up the down conveyor belt. A slow, deep, pugnacious drawl interrupted my motherly panic for my sons' safety.

"I would not do that young man."

We all turned to look at a very large man attached to a very large arm that was holding what appeared to be a very large gun.

I watched as my six foot three, thirty year old, economist son slid back down the conveyor belt like a naughty school boy. "We will have to get a pair of ladders and a big stick" said the now helpful uniformed man. The ladders and stick appeared out of nowhere and his female deputy of an uncertain age was invited by her unchivalrous superior to go up the ladder and poke the offending case.

This she did with peerless aplomb and we were on our way with instructions to "Have a good day" even though by then it was ten pm at night.

We ran with much kerfuffle to the American check in desk to see if we could just make the flight. I did not know but in Toronto we had to go through American border control first.

A ferocious, truculent looking chap with a large moustache held his hand out. "Immigration forms that you filled out on the plane please". We all fished about in our pockets and handed him the by now crumpled forms. "Wrong, Wrong, Wrong," he stated giving us a hard stare. "There are some more over there".

We tried again, three sensible people but over tired and overwrought. "Wrong, wrong, wrong" he said as he placed the forms firmly on the counter "Try again".

By this time I really had dealt with enough and said with a rising, capricious tone "I don't care if I have to live in Toronto for the rest of my life I am not getting on another plane tonight".

We picked up our belongings and our defeated, ever so cranky, group headed off to book on the next flight. "It's going to be another two days before you can get to San Francisco" she said. "Toronto is a fabulous place, why don't you just enjoy?"

CHAPTER 36
There's Dancing In Toronto

If you can't get rid of the skeleton in your closet, you better teach it to dance.
George Bernard Shaw

We all had the best steak we had ever eaten and as we sauntered back to the hotel we made a plan to enjoy the next day. We got up bright and early and found a cheerful taxi driver who would show us the sites. Visiting the museums and galleries and the CN tower, we stopped at the St Lawrence market and bought some keepsakes for the children.

The taxi driver was taking us back to the hotel when he started complaining about the traffic and road closures. "You have come the wrong weekend folks, It's the blasted Gay Pride Parade." Just at that moment the floats started to go past.

Every colour of the rainbow and some you have only imagined decorated each float and filled your senses. Music of every style was being played the only condition seemed to be that it was played loudly. Feathers and fur and faces painted with added jewels and sparklers.

"Oh, let's jump out of the taxi" I said "and see what going on". So began the most fun I have ever had in one afternoon and evening of partying. As I have always said "If something cool appears to be happening, just roll with it! What's the worst that can happen?"

The next day we landed in San Francisco with a bump and the hotel had kindly changed our reservation. We picked up our 4x4 at the airport and made our way to the hotel; we knew where we were going as we had stayed there on previous trips. Grant went for a snooze and James and I went for a drink in the bar.

We were sitting chatting about nothing in particular when Grant made an appearance and we both, very unkindly, burst out laughing. Grant is a very immaculate dresser but he has a blind spot when it comes to sandals. His very trendy, recently purchased, specimens were spoiled by bright white socks pulled up to the knee. He stood looking at us quite sternly and I thought, "Oh no is this going to spoil the day?"

After a moment he smiled and said "What a faux pas, I better go and change". He did and we were on our way.

I love San Francisco. In fact I would go as far as to say it is my favourite place on earth. We headed across to have lunch in Fisherman's Wharf at our favourite restaurant. As we sat by the waterfront we ordered the house lunch and spent nearly two hours savouring the delicious mix of lobster, prawns, mussels and crab. I decided I was on my holidays and enjoyed a glass or two of Zinfandel which grows so beautifully in California.

We have a set of things we do when we are there and it had been cut short by our Toronto trip. So we spent our time looking round China Town, Golden Gate Park and Union Square. We had the obligatory boat ride under the Golden Gate Bridge and around the very spooky Alcatraz. The weather was so cold and windy. I stepped on to the boat looking perfectly elegant with straight hair and a beautifully made up face.

I was forced to meet the sea lions at Pier 39 with a bright red face and very frizzy hair. I could hardly meet their gaze. My favourite thing though is to catch a ride on the cable car system. I never tire of the iconic cable cars going up and down the hills and the musical bell that rings all around the city.

CHAPTER 37
The Fabolous Baker Boys

Life is a lot like jazz…its best when you improvise.
George Gershwin.

One evening, as the weather was so warm and calm, we decided to walk for a while before finding a restaurant. We strolled along the waterfront and then turned into the maze of streets. We were engrossed in our conversation and it was a while before we found our bearings.

In the distance I heard the most perfect piano tinkling and an improvisational style singing voice that mixed jazz with R and B. The song was *My baby just cares for me* by Nina Simone, one of my favourite singers.

I followed the sound and as I rounded a corner I saw a delightful blonde young man singing away to a piano accompaniment. He smiled at me and beckoned me in.

I needed no further encouragement and within seconds I was sitting by his side listening to the music. I looked up and noticed Grant and James had followed me inside. They found a table and in time a waiter brought me a sparkling gin and tonic.

When the music stopped I chatted to the band and discovered that they were music conservatoire students saving for a European tour. The night club manager was a fan and let them play there one night a week. Matt agreed to play my request which was *Lover Man* by Billie Holliday.

I went back to Grant to get some money to give to the musicians. James was killing himself laughing. "What's the matter?" I said "You look like Michele Pfeiffer in the *Fabulous Baker Boys* lying across that piano," was my amused son's reply.

THE LOTUS GENERATION

I was only a little put out as I sauntered back to the trio. I was having such a good time that I hoped my husband and son would keep any opinions to themselves.

Matt the piano player was delighted with my contribution to the fund. He smiled his gorgeous smile and said "Are you here for the Gay Pride Parade tomorrow?"

I could not believe my ears. Was I actually following the Gay Pride Parade caravan around America? I looked up from my reverie and gazed about the dimly lit club. There were gorgeous, perfectly turned out men as far as the eye could see. We had walked so far that we were in San Francisco's gay area.

I felt as though I was in an episode of an Armistead Maupin's *Tales of the City*. I would have like to stay but propriety dictated that it was time for me to take my leave. I gave Matt and his fellow musicians a big hug and wished them all the best for their European tour.

I nodded politely at the assembled crowd and then swung nonchalantly by my companions table "Come on, let's go" I said "I am starving."

We found our way back to Fishers Wharf and stayed out until the early hours eating delicious seafood and reminiscing. The boys had beers and I had several marguerites and flew back to the hotel with wings on my heels.

The next morning we headed for the diner on the corner for a hearty breakfast. We had coffee, fruit juice, bagels, cream cheese, eggs over easy, bacon and a short stack of pancakes with maple syrup. You could not have this every day, but once in a blue moon, delicious.

We packed and said farewell to the hotel staff that were always so accommodating. We collected our very large SVU and soon it was time to leave San Francisco. As we drove over The Golden Gate Bridge I crossed my fingers and hoped I would be back before too long. One could never tire of San Francisco as it seemed to me all human life is there.

We were soon on that famous coastal route as we headed towards Santa Barbara. We had a deadline to make as were due at a fancy party at the country club to celebrate July 4th. We stopped for a light lunch and some petrol at an old Mom and Pop restaurant. The boys headed to order some food and I went to the rest room. As I headed back towards them something caught my eye.

In the shop area where you paid for your petrol there was a very large rag doll in shades of pale pink and pale blue. She was hanging from a hook and stood about five foot tall. She had beautiful blue eyes and freckles just like my granddaughter Ellie.

I do not remember thinking about walking but I was propelled by some unbidden force forward and when it was my turn in the queue I asked politely "Hello there, how much is that big rag doll and where did she come from please?" "Mm" said pop "I will ask Mom"

Mom eventually came through, wiping her hands on her apron. She must have been baking as she had a faint smudge of flour on the end of her nose. She looked like a women who had to work hard but was perfectly content with her lot. She bent her head forward conspiratorially "The doll was made by a Mrs Egan in the next town; I promised I would give her rag dolls a try out to see if they made any money for her. This is the first one so there is not really a price."

We settled on $49 as that would give her a little profit and pay Mrs Egan for her work. I desperately wanted Mrs Eagan's project to be a success. In my imagination she was like a character out of *The Little House on The Prairie.*

In reality she was probably a modern mum with a smartly cut bob and a SUV. My sister-in-law Renee was a glamorous theatre director but never happier than when she was sewing things for her children

Pop was urged to go and get his long stick with the hook on the end and after three attempts and a lot of huffing and puffing the big doll flew smartly down. Mom reached her hand out to break her fall and gently handed her to me. I hugged her and realised with a little dismay that she was quite stiff which might put paid to my plan of rolling her up in my case.

However I was going to have some fun with my travelling companions first. When I tucked my arm through hers she was almost as tall as me. Mom and Pop smiled at me as we set off like mismatched contestants in some crazy three-legged race. I took a deep breath to keep my face straight and walked into the restaurant.

THE LOTUS GENERATION

Grant and James had their heads together chatting as I walked up to them. Nobody said a word as I put the life size rag doll on the seat next to me. I could feel inquisitive glances from the fellow diners piercing my shoulders.

Lunch arrived and we all carried on talking. It was absolutely delicious but there was so much of it to get through. There are lots of differences between Americans, Canadians and the English. I believe one of the big differences is in the embarrassment that the English feel about leftovers.

Americans and Canadian restaurants and diners think you are crazy if you don't take a doggy bag. The English would rather die than walk out of an eatery with a bag of food they have already paid for. If they do pluck up the courage it is always "for the dog."

I have no such compunction and picked up our carton of delicious titbits to go. I arrived at the car and as I was fastening Dolly's seat belt they finally cracked. "What do you think you are doing" said my chortling husband and son "I am taking her home for Ellie." I replied determinately.

I had to buy another suitcase but I managed it and "Big Dolly" still sits with her legs crossed elegantly, on the purple sofa, in my granddaughter's bedroom!

CHAPTER 38
The Big Sur And The Eagles

This land is your land: this land is my land from California to the New York Island. From the red forest to the Gulf Stream waters. This land was made for you and me.

Woody Guthrie.

We were soon on our way on the Pacific Coast Highway-Route One. There is only one album to play on this road and play it we did, on a loop, as we sang along. The Eagles greatest hits include *Hotel California* which we would pass on our spectacular journey. *Tequila Sunrise, Take it easy, Lying eyes and Desperado*......

THE LOTUS GENERATION

The Big Sur is one of the most dramatic coastal rides anywhere in the world. We were heading from San Francisco to Santa Barbara to see Susie and Ross.

Along the section of California's coastline between Hearst Castle and Carmel, North America plunges outwards towards the Pacific Ocean, This tenacious piece of highway clinging to the cliffs is soaring and dramatic.

The blue of the restless Pacific waves match the never ending azure sky. As far as the eye could see white horse waves crashed against the rocks. This breathtaking scenery along this redwood lined stretch of road is so beguiling that you have great fortune if you are the passenger. I pity the driver who has to keep his eyes on the road when all you want to do is staring at nature's bounty.

I love this part of the world and the delicious expectancy of never-ending good weather. My friend Amy was planning her wedding on the Californian coast and conveyed all her plans to me over the phone. Everything from the wedding to the reception was outdoors and to my London ears, listening under a grey sky, this sounded very dangerous. "What happens if it rains?" I suggested.

Her peal of laughter made me feel a little silly. "Don't worry, the weather will be absolutely fine" she assured me.

She was absolutely right as the weather was gorgeous and a wonderful time was had by the assembled company. When I took a little breather from the festivities, a question kept nudging away at my relaxed and slightly wine befuddled brain.

"Why are these people here all so beautiful and seemingly completely relaxed?"

Then it occurred to me that there is something very freeing about good weather. People walk with their shoulders back and their limbs move lightly through the air freely as though the spectre of creaking bones had never existed .You may leave your house in London or Manchester looking gorgeous but freezing wind blowing sideways can soon turn you into a figure from an L.S. Lowry painting in moments.

On the subject of weddings abroad I have been on a decade's long search for a perfect, packable hat. I have bought them in every shape and size only to be so disappointed when a beautiful, packed creation is unpacked as a squished, squashed monstrosity. The only headwear that looked as great when it came out of the case as when it went in was no use at all to me.

The brand new case decided it was not in the mood for a Greek wedding and went on a journey of its own to far away shores.

We travelled to Monterey and stopped at the Black Bear Diner for lunch. Their Huckleberry ice cream is a delicious way to finish a huge meal that will keep you going for hours.

As we drove mile after mile I sometimes had a weird feeling as though I was in an episode of *The Rockford Files* or *Diagnosis Murder* with the familiar beachside views. I kept a keen eye out for Dyke van Dyke or James Garner in the far distance. We had to keep going as our hosts were expecting us go out with them for the July 4th celebrations.

We drove into Santa Barbara as twilight was just descending. Santa Barbara is a picture perfect place located about 90 miles from Los Angeles along the Pacific Coast. It is easy to see why this it's known as the American Riviera as its geography and climate are similar to the Mediterranean coast. The Spanish connection is very clear in the Mission Santa Barbara which is known as The Queen of the Missions and founded in 1786.

CHAPTER 39
The Country Club

A cousin is a readymade friend for life.
Anon.

We drove towards the woodland home of our cousins and to our delight their whole family were waiting to greet us. My husband Grant has lovely four sisters who are a really homogenous group but none of them is anything at all like him.

However, his cousin Susie shows a real family resemblance as they both favour their mothers who were sisters. It was lovely to see her smiling face and see how much her beautiful children had grown.

Ross her husband, who looks like James Bond with his dark hair and urbane manner showed us to our rooms. A quick drink and we were on our way to the country club. The inky blue night sky set off the sparkling lights lining the entrance to the venue for the July 4th celebrations.

There were waiters in crisp white jackets bringing trays of canapés and champagne and everyone was in a festive mood. The children played with their friends and Susie and I had time for a chat. I will always be grateful to her because she provided a wonderful hospitable sojourn for all my children when they were on their back packing journeys of discovery.

A loud bang interrupted our conversation and then the sky was alight with spectacular multi-coloured stars. The firework display was out at sea accentuating the vista of the bay. We sat with the children on our knees admiring the spectacular light show.

As that came to a close the barbeque was offered. There were large platters of chicken, steak and burgers accompanied by salads of every description. The children had sliders with fries and beans which they declared delicious.

James and Ross carried the sleeping children to the car and we set off home. Their timber house in spacious woodland looked picturesque lit up on the hill. The individual tree canopies linked and overlapped so that they gave a complete sward of green. We pulled into the drive and I decided to turn in for the night as I knew a big day was planned for tomorrow. I left the rest of the party enjoying the night air on the terrace.

Ross and his rather patrician father took us out the next day. His father Jed was a lawyer that had ventured into politics and had very firm opinions on absolutely everything. He was a big fan of George W Bush and spent most of the journey singing his praises.

He had very kindly invited us out for the day on his yacht. I am not a big sailor but Max aged six wanted to go and his mother was working so I went along to sit with him. I was really glad I did as it was a perfect sunny day and the Bay was just perfect, calm and seductive.

After three hours sailing around the bay, Jed looked at my son and said "Come on James, you take her in". I frowned and then I sat quietly watching my son sailing the ocean going yacht and thought there are lots of things you don't know about your children's abilities once they are adults.

We had a delicious meal that evening as Susie was an excellent cook. I spent time with the children reading stories and playing games. Millie was as blonde as Max was dark: both as cute as a button. We were going to see their friends the next day so they went to bed happily.

CHAPTER 40
The View From The Beach

Nature's beauty, sea mist and the sound of the ocean on the beach.
Anon.

The next morning we headed to the beach for breakfast and then drove to their friend's house. Susie was a realtor and had just sold her dot com friend a piece of property on the coast. Their plan was to knock the house down and build a new one.

We headed up the drive to an old house on a massive acreage. There were ancient barns and dilapidated out buildings as well as the main house. We were introduced to Mike and his beautiful wife Amina. They had cute twin boys of about six, tall and well built. As they walked towards us I noticed with mirth that they were both wearing white facemasks: they looked like surgeons about to operate.

They put they hands out and spoke in unison "We are very pleased to meet you but we heard that you have been to Toronto and we do not want to take the risk." I took their hands and agreed that was a good safety measure.

Two minutes later Amina called us in for lunch. We sat round the table and started to eat the cold cuts and many salads that had appeared by magic in the dining room. The boys were hungry but they were struggling to eat anything through the masks.

Eventually the older of the identical boys by ten minutes, made a decision and ripped off his mask. "Oh, it really doesn't matter, I am going to risk it" he said to nobody in particular. His brother just copied what he did and their mother took absolutely no noticed of them at all.

After lunch Mike showed us the plans of the house which looked spectacular. He rubbed his hands together and said, "Fancy a trip to the beach?"

We went outside and all jumped in golf buggies that were parked outside the back door.

Then we all set off on a horizontal journey that quickly became terrifyingly vertical. Their private beach was 300 feet below the cliff edge and only accessed by a terrifying zigzag path. We went first this way and then that and to my mind, at a breakneck speed. I squeezed my eyes as hard as I could and prayed for deliverance. Finally we screeched to a shuddering halt.

I opened my eyes to see if everyone had arrived safely. Once I realised that they had, I could begin to relax and enjoy the sunshine and sea view. The company played volley ball and tennis and ran in and out of the water.

Through the sunshine a damp, grey wisp of the mist that sometimes appears in that area, was just beginning to show itself in the distance. Suddenly, a cold, clammy sensation eased itself into my solar plexus as certain knowledge reached my brain: what had come down must eventually go back up.

I tried to be cheery and polite company as everyone enjoyed the beach but soon enough the call to the golf buggies was issued. I found myself sitting in the last one and as I firmly clamped my sweaty palms around the roll bar I closed my eyes for the duration.

There was lots of shouting and hooting as the caravan processed vertically. First this zig and then that zag as we made our way back up to the garden and safety. My companions included me in their conversation but I only had enough air in my body for the act of breathing.

Finally we came to a halt on terra firma and I wished, not for the first time, that my physical being was more a carefree and abandoned version.

We had fresh lemonade in the garden and bade them farewell. We made our way back to Susie and Ross's home and settled in for the night as we had an early start next morning.

There was a bit of a worry the next day as James's had woken up with a huge, red hot left hand. We all stood about peering at it and

THE LOTUS GENERATION

the consensus was that he must have been bitten in the garden at the country club.

Grant, James and I said our goodbyes and promised to see them the next year in the UK. They had been wonderful hosts and made us very welcome. We headed for the nearest pharmacy and James showed them his increasingly throbbing left hand. They all peered at it and the consensus of opinion was that he had been bitten but they did not know by what.

They staff at the chemist were brilliant and prescribed all James needed to repair his hand for the coming few days and we were off on our way to Las Vegas.

CHAPTER 41
The View In The Desert

Man has wrested from nature the power to make a desert or to make the desert bloom.

Adlai Stevenson

It was later than we intended when we left Santa Barbara and we needed lunch before we set off on our journey. We decided to take our burgers to go and soon we were eating up the miles in our SUV.

I must have nodded off and came to, just as the sun was going down. When I looked out of the window I realised I could see aeroplanes stretching into infinity. Reaching for miles and miles into the distance, this was the famous Mojave Desert aeroplane graveyard. The site of some huge planes glinting and glimmering in the late evening sun was breathtaking. They had been piling up there since 9/11 and were used for spares.

As we drove on into the night we spied lights twinkling in the distance and thought for a moment that we might already be at our destination. However it soon became clear that it was a town with a huge shopping mall that was open into the small hours.

Approaching Las Vegas at night from the desert is a spectacularly thrilling experience. The fact that Las Vegas is a construct of Mammon does not take away from the utter heart lifting magic of seeing the sparkling and shimmering edifice stretching out into the night. We were in good spirits and the three of us let out an unexpected cheer and then laughed at our silliness.

Grant has a theory that if you tip people at the beginning of your trip rather than the end you are more likely to get great service. It always seems to work for him. Our hotel was easily recognisable as it had a bright laser beam stretching up into the night sky and can be seen from space. It is of course the Luxor Hotel.

We drove down the strip to experience Vegas at night in all its luminosity. We passed all the big hotels in their glory and The Bellagio with its spectacular botanical gardens and the best "all you can eat" buffet in town, the sophisticated Mandalay and the famous Four Seasons. We marvelled at the fountains outside the palatial Venetian and then decided to go back to our hotel.

James had driven the last leg of the trip and carefully stopped at the front entrance of the Luxor. As he got out and stretched his back, his Dad spoke to the concierge and within seconds the car had been driven away by the valet service and we were being escorted to the check in desk. My attention was soon drawn by the chinking of the slot machines and excited shouting at the dice tables. I looked around and the frenetic activity was overwhelming.

We were escorted to our rooms through the casino and along the travelator. I realised there were no windows anywhere and it felt like I was in outer space. A little shiver went up and down my spine but I decided to breathe and just relax.

CHAPTER 42
The Case Of The Folding Chair

Big Girls need big diamonds.
Elizabeth Taylor

Las Vegas hotel rooms are some of the best in the world and we were quite happy with ours. The chaps went downstairs to have a look around at the hotel whilst I relaxed in a luxurious round bath. I am not a gambler but I love Las Vegas. Anywhere that can provide me with ice cream either day or night gets my vote.

THE LOTUS GENERATION

The next day at breakfast the chaps suggested that they would like to go on a helicopter trip around the Grand Canyon. I declined their offer to go with them and said I was going to do a little sunbathing before having a massage.

I waved them off and packed up my beach bag including towel, book, sun lotion and sunglasses. What more could a girl need? I had never sunbathed before in Las Vegas as I thought it would be too hot.

I tip toed down the marble staircase and sashayed across to the heavy glass doors. I was feeling rather elegant and sophisticated. I had on a beautiful Israeli blue and gold strapless swimsuit with a matching wrap. My sandals had been bought from the same boutique in Italy and were just gorgeous. In fact I felt gorgeous, no contest.

I peered out through the doors and spied row after row of heavy teak sun loungers. There were many more people than I expected occupying the nearer loungers but I spied one empty one not far from the pool. I headed for that one as I made my way outdoors.

The stifling heat hit me like a sledge hammer and I did wonder about turning back as it seemed somewhat overwhelming. I manoeuvred my way carefully through the sunbathers to the lounger I had chosen.

I put my bag down and laid my towel over the hot wooden slats. I put my bottom on the lounger and lay back slowly and tentatively. The next thing I knew I was tumbling and turning and within a split second the heavy wooden contraption had folded up with me in it. I was actually lying face down on the floor with the whole thing on top of me.

In my dizzy state I decided that I was going to lie there until dark as that would be a better alternative to the embarrassment that awaited me if I tried to stand up. After what seemed like a long time a broad Yorkshire voice said "You better go and see if that girl is alright, Ernie". I heard a big sigh and a creaking sound as Ernie got off his lounger.

The next thing I saw as I tried to turn my head was a glimpse of Ernie's sparse hair plastered to his hot, ruddy, bald pate. Then he moved the slats aside and put his whole head in to my vision "Take my hand, love and I will pull you up". Holding back the tears of hysteria I reached out and took his hand. With him pulling and me pushing I managed to get on my feet. "Are you alright love?" said his wife who had sent Sir Galahad to my rescue.

I looked down at my grazed knees and elbows and said "Am I heck all right, a heavy wooden object has just had me pinned to the floor" and then I remembered my manners "but thank you for asking". Then I added "It is fortunate that God gave me a sense of humour" and a smiled a wan smile as I limped back into the hotel.

I could feel hundreds of eyes on me as I caught sight of the grazed, dishevelled wreck that had replaced the perfect goddess of ten minutes ago. I thought about my mother's words "Pride always comes before a fall!" I spent the afternoon putting antiseptic on my injuries and decided not to tell my travelling companions about my adventure.

It only occurred to me on the plane home that the lounger was probably broken and I should have reported it to the authorities rather than blaming myself.

I remembered what I had been told years ago about the difference between boys and girls. If a boy trips up in the playground he looks around to see who pushed him. If a girl trips up in the playground she scolds herself for being so clumsy. The more things change the more they stay the same.

My husband and son had a wonderful day. They had been picked up by a limousine and then flown out of Vegas airport in a helicopter. They had marvelled as they flew over the Hoover Dam and Lake Mead as the scenery was some of the most spectacular that they had ever witnessed. They both agreed the whole trip was worthwhile for that trip alone.

After a few fun days in Vegas we climbed back in the car to drive to our hotel in Santa Monica before catching the plane from Los Angeles to Vancouver for the wedding.

We found our hotel and I opted for a snooze whilst the men went for a walk. When they returned two hours later they had the look of two gambrinous men. Smiling and congenial they had found a wonderful tavern to enjoy the evening air. We walked slowly into the town stopping for a restorative coffee and then enjoyed the evening air and festive environment.

Looking around all the restaurants we decided on the aptly named The Lobster as this is what we intended to eat that evening.

The restaurant was upbeat and the food delicious. We all agreed it was the best lobster we had ever tasted and as we were seated near the window we had a great view as dusk started its slow descent.

The sunset over the water was spectacular with its vibrant shades of pink, orange and red's that faded from view and as darkness fell the lights of the amusement park took over the scene with their garish but strangely hypnotic fascination.

As we left the restaurant we could hear the music of the merry go rounds enticing us to come closer. We walked around and then left the revellers to the night as we had an early start the next day.

CHAPTER 43
We Are Here For A Wedding, Sir!

Happy is the man that finds a true friend, far happier is he that finds that the true friend is his wife.

Franz Schubert

We did some last minute shopping and then headed for LAX for our flight to Vancouver. We returned the car and then took a short taxi ride to the airport. I could not believe it when I saw the queue. It was so long and I thought we were sure to miss our flight. Two seconds later Grant tugged my arm and we were off. He had given $10 to a porter to get our bags from the taxi and he said "follow me." Soon we were heading for the only empty gate and through to the other side in a flash. I was so grateful to him and smiled my thanks.

The flight started off in a very bumpy manner. James was sitting two rows in front of me and turned to remark, "We must have a YTS trainee". I noticed I was the only one that smiled but then I realised that no one else would know what he was talking about.

Eventually we landed and made our way to Immigration. A very tall chap with a nice face that was at odds with his surly manner enquired "Where do you think you are going?" as he looked into my eyes. "I am going to my cousins wedding" I replied politely. "Where is your wedding gift?" he asked, still far too surly for my liking. "In the age of internet shopping, I hope it is already in their beautiful home" was my reply.

At that point Grant gave me a little shove in the back for being lippy. The tall Canadian glared and wondered how he could catch me out. "Where is the wedding being held then?" he said thinking he had really stumped me.

"Ha-ha" I thought I know this one and proceeded to give him directions. I had been to Vancouver so many times that I knew how to get there from down town.

He eventually capitulated and waved the three of us through. We got a taxi to the hotel where the reception was being held and enjoyed meeting all the family who were arriving from all the four corners of the world.

Joshua and Kylie's wedding day dawned cool and bright and an early shower made way for sunshine. The bride was stunning in a white column dress which set off her amazing jet black curls and the bridesmaids colours were perfect shades of pink and red that went together beautifully.

The bride's mother and father walked her down the aisle and then the groom's mother and father accompanied him which gave the whole thing a wonderful family feeling.

The reception was memorable with delicious food and wine and then the happy couple set off on their Italian honeymoon. We were only in Vancouver for forty eight hours but I would not have missed it for the world.

PART TWO

CHAPTER 44
I Think We Need A Change

If you don't like something change it, if you can't change it, change your attitude.

Maya Angelou

In May of 2005 The Labour Party were re-elected to power and the margin of victory was sixty-six seats. Somehow the announcement that Prince Charles was to marry Camilla Parker Bowles created more attention in the press. The wedding took place in April and even the hardest heart could not fail to be moved by a love story that had lasted a lifetime.

The excitement that the whole country felt at being awarded the Olympic Games for 2012 was sadly short lived. Only a day later there was carnage in London as the tube and bus bombs killed fifty innocent people. The whole country reeled in shock and horror at the senseless events of that painful day.

David Cameron was elected leader of the Conservatives and England won the Ashes. The famous footballer and poster boy of sixties coolness, George Best died and set Grant reminiscing about his glory days.

The sounds of Peter Kaye and Tony Christie filled the airways. "Amarillo" was the song for the Children in Need charity and was great in its own right but the video of the song was absolutely hilarious with a favourite, older comedian Ronnie Corbett falling from the escalator. Fortunately he was unhurt and still smiling when he got back on his feet.

For some absolutely unknown reason I started playing The Sugar Babes *Push the Button* if I had to psyche myself up to run a course or do anything that required aplomb and confidence. I am pleased to say it continues to work for me.

In the same vein the two songs that I use to round off training courses have always been Queen's anthem *Don't stop me now* and Paul Weller's *Shout to the Top*.

THE LOTUS GENERATION

To me these songs say, "Let's express our joy, let's dance, we've had a great experience and now it's time to go home".

Musical anchors are powerful things.

My husband Grant had been quiet and distracted since we came back from our wonderful grand tour. I however was determined to concentrate on my work as I had been on a lot of trips and needed to have a period of determined hard work.

After about a month of wondering what was wrong I sat him down and said "Do you have a problem and if you do, can I help?" My husband had always needed change and excitement and I really wondered what was wrong with him.

He had not worked since his heart attack and I had tried hard to be supportive but I felt in the end he had to find the answer for himself. I knew he had heard the ticking of the clock since his heart bypass operation and needed to feel young again even though he was only just in his fifties.

You could have knocked me over with a feather when he smiled and then said "I want to go travelling. Let's buy a camper van and take off for five years."

Gosh, was I was sorry that I had asked?

He stood up with a flourish and said "Life is for living!" Flourishing was not his style so I wondered what was going on in his head.

We talked into the night and the next day we went looking at camper vans.

I am nothing if not a trooper.

In the end this was dismissed as a fantasy but within two weeks he had come up with another way around domesticity and suburban living.

"Let's rent the house out and go and live in Spain for a year."
I lay awake all night pondering his latest plan and in the small dark hours came to the conclusion that it just might work.

I was self-employed so I could work anywhere and I thought my private counselling and coaching work would be transportable. I did a lot of telephone coaching and I had done that from wherever I was in the world. The only downside was that my daughter had two young children but she also had a good husband and lots of help in the house.

I promised her I would be back every two weeks and I tried to keep that promise for the whole time I was away. When I rang my sister, to run the plan by her, she was delighted and she soon found us a beautiful apartment near where she lived.

Within a month I had to sit down and make a decision whether I was going to really go on the adventure or not. I sat down with a piece of paper and wrote down the good and the not so good sides of a year in Spain.

In the end it came down to this, who was I going to please?

CHAPTER 45
We Are Off On A Gap Year

They must often change, who would be constant in happiness and wisdom.
Confucius

I lay awake night after night but after much soul searching I finally decided to go to Spain with Grant and soon our family home was rented out and we were off on the plane to Alicante.

I travelled on that plane route so many times over the next three years that I became the most golden of the gold card customers. We kept our car at the airport and could be home door to door in less than three and a half hours.

I soon came to love the country, the people and the way of life. Somehow, everything changed in those first few months. A magical horologist enabled the clock to tick backwards and miraculously we became young again.

Humans are very resilient and the unfamiliar becomes the familiar in a heartbeat. For us living in suburbia and the occasional visit to the cinema was replaced by going out every night, even if it was just for a walk on the beach to see the setting sun.

A laissez faire attitude prevailed and the diktat that lunch was at 12.30pm and supper at 6.30pm was replaced by an anything goes disposition that lunch was around 3pm and supper was a moveable feast anywhere between 9pm and midnight.

I had cooked a meal every day of my life since I was a child but in this new Shangri-La eating out was a daily pleasure and there was always someone you knew in whatever restaurant you chose.

The Menu Del Dias was just a few euros and in the part of the country in which we lived it was almost certainly traditional delicious Spanish fare with a bottle of wine thrown in for good measure!

My group of friends in the UK are all like me and I loved them all and felt safe and comfortable with them. Most of my group of friends and colleagues in Spain are nothing like me and they began to stretch my whole being emotionally and spiritually.

I made friends with people of all ages from all over the world and every day was an adventure. I counted Dutch, Swedish, Norwegians, Australians, South and North Americans as well as Spaniards amongst my best friends. If people did not have much money they bartered their skills, a coaching course for translation help, yoga lessons for cooking for the freezer and therapy sessions for Spanish lessons.

I woke up every morning with the sun beating down, full of endless possibilities for my life.

I quickly built up a client base and worked long hours until late into the evening, as afternoon in Spain lasts until eight pm. I worked at a clinic about forty minutes away on the coast and loved that sun drenched journey up and down the motorway. There was a deep sense of spirituality in that beautiful corner of the world.

Grant relaxed and spent his days walking on the beach. Ten miles a day was no problem for him and he began to believe he could live for ever. Tanned and fit his mood lifted and I heard him laugh again

We made friends in the drop of a hat and my brother-in-law Malcolm introduced me into the local business community. My nephew, who was at law school, spent a lot of time with his parents and we enjoyed his company. One day I asked him if he would help me with something on the computer and patient as ever he spent three days making sure I knew what he knew. This meant that months later I knew enough to set up an online retail business.

THE LOTUS GENERATION

My children and grandchildren came out to visit regularly but I could see in my children's eyes that they really did not recognise the people their parents were becoming…..

There is a metaphorical elephant in the room that stands between early middle aged children and their late middle aged parents.

The elephant looks bit like this…....

A generation that is now early in early middle age has had a wonderful time with long university education, backpacking around the world and child free years when they could party all night and stay in bed all day. Child rearing is definitely harder when you have been used to having time for yourself.

A generation that is now in late middle age had those children when they were in their early twenties. They still want to enjoy culture, look good, travel, party and have fun. Most parents who are sixty plus now adore their grandchildren and children and would do anything for them but still see themselves as vibrant human beings who intend to keep on dancing...

We all need to give each other a break and understand that life really is changing and for the better….

CHAPTER 46
Music, Joy And Fireworks

The world is a book and those who do not travel read only a page.
St. Augustine

The temperature in Great Britain soared and reached 36 degrees at Wisley, our favourite place for a walk. The water restrictions played havoc with gardens both private and municipal. I began to hear discussion of changing planting displays to meet the prospect of a changing dryer climate. I was asked many times about designs in Spain a country of low rainfall.

I began to realise that Spain is a country of music, joy and colour. Soon you begin to appreciate the glorious sounds coming from whatever building you are passing. In homes, churches and schools someone was always practising their instrument or you could hear a choir is being put through its paces.

The tree lined marble main street of the town we lived in was a long, elegant and sophisticated boulevard to the sea. In my experience contemporary Spanish women are always beautifully groomed with lovely hair and clothes and so their jewellers and hairdressers are on every corner. Upscale boutiques and fantastic shoe shops merge into chemists and banks as you go about your business. Coffee shops and restaurants spill out onto the pavement to make the most of the sunshine.

The hardest thing I had to get used to be the idea of shops closing for at least two hours at lunchtime and being open until late into the night. The sound of voices is always in the air and people love to stop and chat with their friends and neighbours. Life is the same whether it is light or dark outdoors and small children go everywhere with their parents. As in 1950s Britain the older children look after the smaller ones and it is common to see seven year olds responsible for their younger siblings.

Every evening there was a reason to go out and in the spring after we arrived it was the time of the Falles. This traditional fiesta marks St Joseph's day which is also Father's day in Spain.

The history of this festival stems from the carpenters who used to rest their candles on a plank of wood in the winter and then burn the plank when spring came around.

Ninots are huge, intricate papier-mâché and plaster life like statues that have been lovingly made by local associations throughout the year. When they are filled with fireworks they are described as Fallas and remain in place until the evening of the burning which is called the Crema.

Some of these papier-mâché statues are as tall as three story buildings and the dignitaries of the town go around in a procession and score them on creativity and interest. Then they are burned in the order in which they came in the competition so that the best is saved until last.

When the competition is over the street lights are turned off and the handsome young bomberos take their places.

Along with most countries I have been to visit I was sure the firemen here in Spain had to pass some sort of invisible handsome test before they are allowed to wear the uniform, Brave and composed they begin to soak the surrounding buildings with jets of water and the statue is set on fire.

As this was the first festival we had attended there was no way to be prepared for the scintillating flashes and clamorous bangs. The street lights went off, the crowd started to chant and flames rose into the air illuminating the dark night.

Then just when you thought that was enough fireworks started flying out in all directions. Flaming paper drifted to the ground and landed on whatever it touched and continued to burn. It was impossible to move as the crowd was so dense. I had to really take control of myself to stop fear overtaking me.

I closed my eyes and could feel my sister's grip pinching my arm through my coat. After we managed to escape from the crowd into the cooler air we found a stall selling churros and thick hot chocolate which we consumed happily on our way home.

I said quite categorically, "I shall never, ever go to that challenging conflagration again".

However after some time living in Spain I was as insouciant as the next person about the raining flames and shaking earthquake sensations and sounds as the next person.

CHAPTER 47
Please Don't Throw Me Over Your Shoulder

Dancing with the feet is one thing, dancing with the heart is another?
Anon.

In the shadows I could just about make out some luminous writing on the back wall. It was in Spanish so I could not make out the meaning. A cool dry hand took mine and a voice whispered "Hurry up" and began to pull me along down a corridor.

I was tired, testy and somewhat disorientated as I had been travelling on a long journey back from a wedding in Scotland. As I looked around in the stygian gloom I could just about make out shapes that may have been people up against the wall.

Some people appeared to be sitting and some of them standing and they were speaking in hushed, desultory tones. I looked back to see if my husband Grant was behind me but there was no sign of him. Suddenly the cool hand let go of mine and I was stood helpless and disorientated in an unknown space. My ears heard the crash of chords before my eyes saw the flashing lights.

"Ah well common everybody and let's get together tonight, *I got some money in my jeans* and *I am really gone to spend it right....*"

At the sound of Eddie Cochran's first iconic guitar chord the fifty or so couples that had been lounging round the edge of the room were stung into action and commenced rock and rolling with frankly amazing vigour.

A chap with a friendly face to whom I had not yet been introduced put a gin and tonic in my hand and said charmingly,

"Welcome to your first rock and roll dance."

As I looked round and saw my sister and her friend Jenny who was the Queen of rock and roll. Jenny wore a white Marilyn Monroe style dress and had beautiful blonde curls. She was the owner of the cool hand that had welcomed me.

Whilst my sister had been in Spain she had as always had made lots of friends. When we were alone I whispered "I am too young to do this rock and roll stuff and you are younger than me so what gives?"

"Don't be such a killjoy "she whispered back sharply "This is great fun" and she was off, twirling and bouncing up and down in time to the music with her pals.

I had expected this evening in Spain to be tapas and classical guitar not Eddie Cochran and Duane Eddy in the Black and White nightclub. I leaned across to my less than pleased husband and co-driver from England.

"Well, if you can't beat them....." I yelled as I kicked my shoes off and whirled into tangled mass of Spanish and English dancers jiving away to their hearts content.

A very nice man helped me with my first steps and as I got more confident he twirled me first this way and that. The music was

THE LOTUS GENERATION

life affirming and I began to get into the swing of things. Eventually he said "If you are feeling confident my next move will lift you right up in the air".

I stopped dead in my tracks and looked at him with tears of mirth running down my by now very red face "Gosh, good luck with that one mate, I think I better go and sit down"

When I took my place at a table with my husband Grant and brother-in-law Malcolm neither would meet my gaze and that made me laugh even more.

My sister Gillian is so glamorous, she always has been and I imagine always will be. Blonde perfectly coiffured hair, nails elegant, painted just the right colour and makeup applied with the kind of dexterity that I could never hope to replicate. Her clothes and jewellery were always immaculate and she was never seen without her trademark four inch heels.

About three months after we arrived in Spain my sister and I booked jiving lessons with some local Spanish champions. We danced around the school hall with our husbands and could not even get the simple command "Bread Basket!" correct.

However, whenever we changed dancing partners we found our level of expertise went up dramatically.

With our tapping feet halted for a moment and our bosoms still jigging up and down to Eddie Cochrane's *Common Everybody* my sister and I had a mini conference.

We decided there and then that it was our husbands that could not dance and actually we were quite satisfactory rock and rollers, thank you very much.

CHAPTER 48
The Way And The Swan

Everything has beauty, but not everyone sees it.
Confucius

That summer floods caused chaos in the West Country and we were glad that the Climate Change Bill had set targets for big changes. In July the smoking ban in England arrived and crowds of people were to be seen standing outside offices, bars and nightclubs.

We wondered how the ban would affect the Spaniards as there seemed to be many more smokers there.

I was with a group of women friends eating pastries and drinking cortados at a café one morning. We were outside sitting at elegant tables but part of the floor was glazed so that the ancient town walls on which it was built were visible.

One of our party lit a cigarette and several of the black clad staff ran, wildly gesticulating, to remonstrate with her in no uncertain terms. Carmen is Spanish so she gave as good as she got but all her entreaties were in vain. The argument that she was really outside cut no ice with any of them. I never actually saw anyone smoke inside after the ban.

We loved watching Jools Holland and his music show on BBC2. I had seen him a few times years ago with the group Squeeze and enjoyed his promotion of young artists. We saw a teenager called Adele Adkins and both said that we thought she was wonderful and that we thought we would see her again.

Watching "Later with Jools Holland" on BBC Two and listening to Paul Weller, Amy Whitehouse and the host's rendition of *Don't go to Strangers* reduced me to tears sitting on my Spanish veranda one balmy evening.

I really had no idea why I was crying, it just touched something deep within my soul and it continues to do so to this day.

We lived near a gym where all the beautiful people hung out. It was a source of great amusement to me that folks that could spend two hours manically spinning on fixed bikes would fight to get the car

THE LOTUS GENERATION

space nearest to the gym, so they did not have to walk for a moment longer than necessary.

Jennifer was the beautician who ran the spa and salon in the gym. Her parents had lived in Spain for twenty-five years so she was as Spanish as she was English. Her cheerful demeanour and tinkling laugh made her a delight to be with.

She was up to date with all the treatments she offered and I was frankly willing to give anything a go. I worked long hours and so when I went once a month she managed to do everything in two hours. She had a machine that tightened your waist but hurt like hell but in my mind one thing was commensurate with the other.

I loved to enter that deliciously scented space and just give myself up to the relaxation. One day as I walked into the spa to the sound of whale music and the sight of candles flickering, I felt so tired.

I climbed up on the table and the last thing I remember was Jennifer gently applying a moisturising mask to my feet before I fell fast asleep.

I was startled awake by a feeling that can only be described as a demented swan pecking my middle and I screamed very loudly. Poor Jennifer had been completely relaxed as she was leaning over me applying a scented face balm. She was jolted alarmingly out of her reverie.

The shock of her client screeching set her off and soon we were both yelling. "What is the matter? Whatever is the matter?" she said with rising alarm.

"Something terrible …. is biting, me," I replied fighting hysterically to get out of the heated layers she had wrapped me in.

Eventually we both stared at the contraption that had caused the shock. The waist cinching machine that she put on automatic timer for the last half hour had caused the problem as it had woken me out of a deep sleep.

I was on my feet by then and we both decided that abandonment of the session would be appropriate.

I hugged her, paid her in euros and set off home for a medicinal Spanish brandy with my coffee.

THE LOTUS GENERATION

When I got back home the television news was running clips of President George Bush greeting Prime Minister Tony Blair with a cheery "Yo, Blair." I really could not see what was wrong with it as they were obviously good pals. However it seemed everybody had an opinion on the incident and was going to voice it!

In the horrendous storms that lashed the Spanish coast that summer Jennifer was riding on the back of a quad bike. The day had started out sunny and soon took a turn for the worse. A freak wave swept her out to sea and it was only the bravery of a local Spanish man that saved her from certain drowning. It was a dreadful ordeal and although she came back to work months later there was something about the light in her eyes that had changed.

A small child called Madeline went missing in Portugal that summer and we all felt the pain of her bereft and desolate parents.

Chapter 49
Fun In The Sun

Those who bring sunshine into the lives of others cannot keep it from themselves.

J.M. Barrie

The crowd of friends that my sister had made were wonderful and included us in their plans immediately. There was a plan every single day. A women's group, a salsa class, a sailing class or a chess club were just a few that were available.

We were invited out every single evening. There were formal functions, dances, restaurant dinners, supper parties and barbeques on the beach.

There always has to be a leader in any group and Jenny the rock and roll queen was the definite leader in this group. Always immaculate she never sat down as she was convinced that would be the ruination of her figure. She was married to an older man Paul and basked in his adoration. They were always friendly whenever you saw them strolling along the beach hand in hand.

Marion and her husband Bill were the kindest and funniest of the group. They had both been probation officers in England and after

THE LOTUS GENERATION

their eyes met over a table at a conference they had been inseparable. Marion loved swimming and could often be found whizzing up and down the pool at the gym in the early hours of the morning.

Rita and James had a beautiful home in the hills with the most English of gardens. He lived just to make sure that her life was perfect and smiled at anything she said. Kind hearted but plain spoken she would very often give you her opinion whether you wanted it or not. They only ever danced with each other no matter where we were.

In the group was a couple so devoted that they even talked in unison. Ginny and Derek seemed the most constant of all our friends and I think were the best salsa dancers.

John who was married to Margaret spent most of his time in the air as he was still working as an engineer in the Middle East.

However there were lots of different couples and singletons in the group so no one was alone and the whole crowd was very supportive of each other in the way of expats all over the world.

Another friend who I met through my sister was the young woman who did our nails. Lisle was originally from Germany and had lived all over the world. In New York she married a man from Uruguay and had six children in quick succession. She was beautiful and mercurial and she enjoyed the buzz of city life in America. However when they moved back to Uruguay she found it did not suit her and the whole family then moved to Spain and her marriage did not survive the upheaval,

She worked like a Trojan every day getting her children ready for school in a morning, doing women's nail extensions all day then running back to get the children their supper.

As the evening drew in her working day began as she ran her Dutch boyfriend's popular restaurant. It was popular but only because she was sunny and fun and made people welcome.

Intelligent and fluent in seven languages she fell in bed about three am ready to be up at six am ready to go again. Her never failing Joy de vivre and energy was contagious.

CHAPTER 50
What Can I Do With A Jar Of Quince Paste?

Sometimes I've believed as many as six impossible things before breakfast.
Lewis Carroll

Grant adored the beach and the sound of the ocean and so every morning he loved to go for a long walk down to the Los Angeles hotel in the next village. Sometimes I would jump in the Land Rover and meet him at this very swish hotel for breakfast. The proprietors forbade sand in their immaculate hotel so beach lovers would sit outside in the lushly planted gardens watching the tiny fishes darting about in the pool. It was so peaceful; sitting under the palm trees sipping delicious coffee con leche and eating a typical Spanish breakfast of cheese, ham and rolls.

We shopped every morning at the indoor market. Every stallholder in this colourful and charming place became a treasured ally. The pretty young raven haired woman whose stall was near the door, sold dried fruits and nuts of every description.

The counter was full of pots of membrillo, the quince paste that is so beloved by every Spanish housewife. She was convinced my sister and I were twins which made her giggle every time we saw her.

The old building was full of butchers selling cuts of meat I did not recognise at first and many different kinds of delicious Spanish cured meats such as jamon iberico, chirizo and butifarra.

The bakers in their white hats had risen at the crack of dawn to fill their stalls with amazing baked goods. Delicious Empanadillas are the Spanish version of the Cornish pasty but filled with fragrant tomato and tuna filling. Eaten warm with a lunchtime glass of beer they are so tasty. The brick shaped salty loaves of dense bread that tasted so delicious when dipped in virgin olive oil, were my favourite daily purchase.

The high glass ceiling was a prism that sent shards of light that bounced off the voluptuous fruit and vegetable stalls. Single avocados and aubergines shone like precious jewels in the mid-day sun.

At the back door of the indoor market the fish sellers reigned supreme. Every startling variety of fish in the Mediterranean Sea was available for purchase. The Spanish housewives seemed to prize

THE LOTUS GENERATION

above all else the tiny bright red prawns that tasted so sweet in soups and paellas. Every single stall sold the ubiquitous, red and yellow jars of paprika of the sweet or smoked variety.

I bought my meat, bread and local honey in the market but it was outside in the sunshine that I spent most of the housekeeping. As you get excited the ancient building it took a few seconds for your eyes to refocus. After a moment's hesitation on the marble steps you were outside in a vast magical world of colour and sound.

Different kinds of fruit and vegetable filled every stall. Fat, juicy oranges still attached to their verdant leaves, alongside lemons as big as tennis balls and then the delicious fruit of the area, the soft peachy coloured apricots.

Between the large commercial fruit stalls were tiny tables covered with lace clothes. The elderly, black garbed, rural lady sold tiny bunches of exquisitely scented flowers as well as herbs, garlic and strings of hot red chillies.

The feather strewn warm brown eggs from hens that scratched out a living on their tiny plots of land were in demand by the early shoppers. If you arrived after eight am you had to make do with supermarket eggs and the flavour of your crema catalane was compromised.

The cost of all this bounty of herbs, fruit and vegetables was miniscule because at the time the exchange rate was defiantly weighted in the Briton's favour.

The sea front was only two minutes' walk from the market and that was where the fishing boats were landed. It was always a thrill to watch the catch being sorted and the fishermen's skill as they jumped on and off the boats. Then the myriad species of glistening fish went straight through to the wholesale market.

There was a high glass viewing balcony and it was fun to take our visitors there to watch the theatre of the bounty of the sea.

We bought all our fish from the shop attached to this place. Our favourite variety was rape or monk fish. I quickly learned the Spanish for "No thank you, I really do not want this" as we were always encouraged to take the enormous head for stock as well as the delicious tail meat.

Monk fish fillets wrapped in salty Iberico ham and baked in white wine with tarragon and green grapes are delicious. Served with crusty bread and a ripe tomato and shallot salad it is ambrosia.

CHAPTER 51
Malcolm And The White Lion

Keep the circus going inside you, keep it going, don't take anything too seriously; it'll work out in the end.

David Niven

My brother-in-law had semi-retired when he moved to Spain but had got bored and looked for a job. The job he found was working for a Spanish company selling whirl pools and spas. His office was situated near a large park. His office door, which he needed to keep open to catch the breeze, faced the entrance to the park.

Spanish circuses are different to British ones. They still have the animal acts that were phased out here in Britain in the 1950s. Consequently any Spanish circus worth its salt had a full complement of lions, tigers, bears, elephants and giraffes. In fact there was more or less one of everything that Noah had taken in his ark in every single circus.

One day we went to see him in his office and I noticed that behind his office chair was a large stick. "What is that for" I said nodding in the chair's direction. Have a look at the local paper he said. I rifled across his desk but could only find a Spanish copy. My capacity to learn the language had proved to be less adequate than his and I asked him to translate.

"Look, look," he said, "The circus is coming back to town and they are bringing that huge white tiger with them again". " Oh," was my inadequate reply. "The trouble is that flimsy cage they keep it in is always parked about ten feet from my office so this time I am ready for him."

We all smiled as we contemplated Malcolm being chased by a white tiger through the streets of the town. We were prepared for the bull running every summer but not tigers at any price.

About two weeks later we were passing the park, as it was near where we lived. We had just got back from the airport and I had wound my window down because the cool night air was like wine after being cooped up in the plane. We stopped for a moment in the traffic. Grant said quietly to me "Don't look now but there is a giraffe with its head in your window."

I turned sharply to look or I would have done if the giraffe had not had its head in the way. I gasped and smiled politely and she batted her lashes and lifted her beautiful head up and away from me, up and away where the air was more rarefied.

I looked at my husband and said, "Life sure is more fun here in Spain than it ever was in the Home Counties". I had been nearer more wild animals in my time in Spain than at any time previously. Whatever happened to me I remembered my motto "If it looks like something cool is going to happen just roll with it. What's the worst that can happen?" He nodded his silent agreement and drove on as the road cleared.

When I told Ellie about my experience she reminded me that the giraffe could not have complained even it wanted to as "Giraffes are the only animals in the whole universe that do not have voice boxes, Granny. Didn't you know that?"

CHAPTER 52
The Moors And The Christians

I have a memory like an elephant. In fact elephants often consult me.
Noel Coward

You cannot escape the feeling that you are a participator in a Middle Age spectacular when the time for the Moors and Christians Festival arrives each year.

This can be any time in spring or summer, depending which part of Spain you live in as the costumes are shared countrywide by the participants. The costumes are mostly ancient and very expensive and so are treasured by each person that wears them.

The festivities date back to the hostilities that took place between the Moors (Muslims) and Christians between the eighth and fifteenth centuries. They particularly commemorate the battles that took place between the Moorish and Spanish soldiers in the thirteenth century for absolute control of Spain.

The festivities last for about a week with the centrepiece being the three hour parade through the town. The atmosphere begins to build on the morning of festival day as the streets are closed off and thousands of chairs are delivered and set out on the pavements.

The bars and cafes bring out coffees and drinks to their customers and you can hear the incessant chatter of the thousands of local people and tourists alike. The first thing you notice is the faint drumbeat of the band as it resonates through your whole being The sound silenced the hushed chatter in a simultaneous heartbeat.

Just as the anticipation appears to be never ending the first magnificent black stallion arrives with its splendidly clad rider so high above the crowd and then following him other horsemen dressed as Christians.

The Christians are covered in fur with amour and their shining metallic helmets gleam and glint in the evening sun. They fire their loud arquebuses, the heavy portable guns invented in the fifteenth century.

Then suddenly the first marching band appears. The bands travel from all over Spain to join in the festivities.

You can hardly believe your eyes as a group of huge brown and cream camels, with their large doe like eyes and their double fringed lashes, come next.

The Moors are wearing splendid, ancient Arab costumes and hoisting heavy gleaming scimitars aloft.

The festival is a joy for adults and children alike as the Christians on stallions and the Moors on elephants or camels are interspersed with other floats. Brass bands playing Marchas Pasadobles and huge floats of local people dressed in traditional costume drive slowly by.

The joyous sounds of cheering and clapping rings out continuously, as each participant passes in the parade. I loved the sight of grown men in their costumes holding the smallest member of their family aloft for the crowd to admire. The woman and girls wear typical medieval costumes of red, green and gold with full skirts and headdresses.

In the provinces of Valencia where we lived and of Alicante further down the coast the festivals were the most glorious in all of Spain. Our home overlooked the village of Villajoyosa where the festival is regarded as the most spectacular event in the area. The fireworks on the hill went on for hours.

The best part about all of this was the fact that every family member was out and about in an evening. It seemed to me that the teenagers were just as likely to meet their Abuela or grandmother out on a Saturday night as their friends and they adjusted their behaviour accordingly.

CHAPTER 53
Working In The Sunshine

Keep your face to the sunshine and you cannot see a shadow.
Helen Keller

My colleague Francesca and I were holding a training course and the hotel we usually used was closed for renovations. A mother of two she was warm and inclusive and she had a beautiful home near the sea and a garden full of fragrant orange and lemon trees.

Although she was much younger than me we got on famously from the day we met and we found working together was fun and creative. When she kindly suggested that we use her house for the course I readily agreed.

We had about twelve people on the coaching course and it was a delightful two weeks. Every morning we woke up to sunshine streaming through the windows and the scent of oranges on the breeze wafting through the windows.

We met for early morning breakfast on the terrace near the pool. Gilda who was our interpreter ran yoga classes at seven am and everyone joined in stretching and setting themselves up for the day.

We had classes in the morning under the cool of the Cenador. Then a delicious lunch brought in each day by a different member of the group. The various tapas, cassoulets, salads and rice dishes meant we ate like Kings and Queens as we sat and exchanged the most pleasant stories and vignettes. Laughter rang around the garden as the all the people made fast friends.

On every Spanish event I ever planned it was critical to leave at least two hours for lunch as there was much to be gained from these nourishing events.

Afternoons were indoors in the cool of the shade and the assembled company settled to learning the skills that would enhance their careers. Afternoon in Spain goes on into the evening and so it was mostly dusk when everyone made for home.

The clinic that I worked at was run by a Scandinavian couple who adored each other and provided a wonderful space for people of all nationalities to have a pleasant space to work. I made a lot of friends there and regard the two years I worked there as some of the most productive working years of my life.

CHAPTER 54
The Ibiza Adventure

Ibiza is always a good idea.
Anon.

Where the tree lined boulevard meets the sea and just along from where the fishing boats land there was always a queue. The snaking line of cars and people were waiting in the shimmering heat for the gleaming white ferry to take them to Ibiza.

One summer morning we decided to join them and had already booked our tickets to the sunny island. The sun drenched three hour journey passed uneventfully and very soon we were disembarking in San Antonia.

The Balearic Island which is a fifth the size of its neighbour Majorca and is best known now for its night life and club scene and thousands of young and not so young people head there every summer to dance the night away.

However we were on a trip to discover the real Ibiza and after hiring a car were on our way. We were off to spend the night in Ibiza old town. This has been declared a UNESCO world heritage site and has a population of about 25,000 people.

Although Spaniards and Britons alike call this place Ibiza its official Catalan name is Elvissa. It is divided into two parts, the old town located on a small mountain by the sea and the modern part which is called Example which simply means the extension.

We found a picturesque white hotel overlooking the deep blue sea and left the car behind to explore our surroundings on foot. We stopped at the first bar to have café con leche and restorative Spanish brandies all round. We were travelling with my sister Gillian and her husband as we usually did as they were such good company.

They were both fluent in the Spanish language whilst we were struggling. I understood every word that was either spoken or written and had sat in on many Spanish language only meetings. However when it came to having a conversation by the time I had marshalled my thoughts the moment had passed.

We had just employed a German lady Beatrix to give us intensive lessons so she was coming to our home three times a week. One evening I could feel a headache coming on and so I took to my bed. I lay there listening to my English husband being coached in Spanish by a jolly but determined German lady and I got the giggles.

I had to put the pillow over my head so they could not hear me laughing. When Grant came to bed he was very pleased with how the lesson had gone and I did not dare tell him that I had found it so amusing. Beatrix kept coming and eventually our Spanish improved dramatically.

We had our first meal on the Island that evening. A monkfish and red pepper starter, lamb cooked long and slow with fat, sweet red tomatoes and the huge butter beans that are available all over Spain for main course. Malcolm was the only one that wanted a pudding and so I kindly agreed to join him in a dish of Arroz con leche. That was until I realised it was a rice pudding, but the honey ice cream that accompanied the dish was sublime.

We made our way to watch the glorious sunset at Ses Variades. There were large crowds there that night to experience the view. The setting orange sun seems to turn the sea into a titian cloudscape of fire.

THE LOTUS GENERATION

The next day we were up and about early as it was Sunday and we wanted to see The Iglesia de Sant Rafel. This little church is on top of the mountain in San Rafael and the views are amazing. The service was an inclusive communal worship and the choir of adults and children alike was exquisite. The four parts of the choir alto, soprano, tenor and bass were easily discernible in this magical setting and the choir richly deserved its description of heavenly.

We wandered out into the sunshine and realised that the church was near the Museo Puget which was next on our agenda.

This museum was only founded in 2007 and celebrates the legacy of Ibiza Narcis Puget Vinas and his son Narcis Puget Vinas. There are lots of watercolours and oil paintings to enjoy from the nineteenth and twentieth century.

Sunday lunch of delicious Paella and a snooze awaited and I am sorry to say the rest of our Ibiza adventure was spent eating and sleeping with the occasional evening of drinking and dancing thrown in for good measure.

CHAPTER 55
The Choir From King's College

I always try to cheer myself up by singing when I'm sad: turns out my voice is worse than my problems.

Anon,

Five minutes' walk from our Spanish home was a marble walkway where there were art shops on one side and a beautiful, gleaming white convent was situated on the other. The windows were high and barred and occasionally as you were walking by you would catch a glimpse of an elderly pale face under a stiff starched wimple.

Once or twice a year they would hold a concert inside the convent but we always seemed to be visiting family in the UK. One year a dear friend bought us tickets as a treat and we were delighted as we took our seats to discover it was Kings College, Cambridge Choir. It was a magical evening and from what we could see of the elderly nuns behind their grill enjoyed it too. The programme was

THE LOTUS GENERATION

Mozart, Haydn and Brahms and with the acoustics in the convent the sound was flawless.

Afterwards we left the convent we walked to the sea and then stopped for drinks at the Buddha Bar before walking out to sea along the harbour. It was a warm but cloudy evening so there were few stars in the sky. As we strolled along the harbour wall we could see hundreds of red lights dancing in the night sky like glow worms at a fancy dress party.

The slapping sound of the waves colliding gently with the harbour wall became more intense as we strolled nearer to the sea.

We stopped for a moment to get our bearings as the bobbing red lights were a little disconcerting. "I know," said Grant, "Its hundreds of fishermen with lights on the end of their rods. They bob about when they cast off."

As we came upon them we could see they were fishing, listening to the radio and drinking local wine in the spirit of bonhomie. Apparently Saturday night is alright for fishing in that part of the Spanish Coast.

There is always a festival somewhere even if you are not expecting one. We went for dinner the next Saturday night and we got more than we expected. The main street was cordoned off and huge paella pans were atop the sweetest smelling wood fires scattered everywhere. Men, both young and old in starched white aprons were stirring these delicious mixes of rice, saffron and rabbit. We lived in the Valencia Province and so historically rabbit was always included in any paella.

A self-important looking band of elders walked up and down the boulevard with their hands behind their backs. They stopped occasionally to stir, sniff and then taste the bubbling brews. Frankly to the untrained eye every pan looked exactly the same but the crowds ran between one and another enjoying the spectacle.

Eventually the committee climbed the wooden stairs to the stage and announced in reverse order, the winners. Two gorgeous local young men who were the crowds favourite were presented with the weighty cup. Paper plates of paella arrived in our hands as if by magic and politeness dictated that they had to be consumed there and then.

THE LOTUS GENERATION

As we had already eaten we repaired to our favourite bar and several alcoholic drinks and a coffee later we wandered back into the warm, starry night. There was music coming from somewhere and as we followed the sound we came across the wooden stage that had been inhabited by the paella judges earlier in the day. To our delight there was a live band of musicians and a beautiful, voluptuous singer who sounded just like Gloria Estefan.

We danced to every kind of Latin music with a few rock numbers thrown in for good luck that night. As we walked home at three am we realised that we had eaten and been entertained by the citizens of that wonderful town, that we were lucky to call home, for those few short years in our lives.

CHAPTER 56
Who Has A Good Time On New Year's Eve?

A New Year's resolution is something that goes in one year and out the other.
Anon.

I love Christmas, all the planning and the shopping and the cooking. I look forward to it for months; however New Year's Eve is another matter. I have often wondered who has a good time then.

For ten years in England we had spent the evening with our neighbours and it had been perfectly delightful. Every year it was at a different house, but the same food, games and conversation ensued. We were always back home and in bed for one a.m. but I always had the feeling there was a great party going on somewhere else. I just had not been invited to it.

My feelings chimed with my favourite Spanish saying. "Esta Noche es Noche-Bueno, Y no Es noche de dormer" Simply translated, "Tonight is a good night and it is not meant for sleeping"

Christmas in Spain is all about family and is usually a quieter more religious affair than in the UK. Felix Navidad or Happy Christmas is on every poster and the billion euro lottery El Gordo on December 22nd starts the feeling of excitement in the air.

THE LOTUS GENERATION

Christmas Eve is called Nochebuena and is an important family occasion. A celebratory meal at home with bubbling Cava to drink can be either turkey or roast meat but there is always seafood as a starter. This meal is usually eaten before midnight mass but is likely to be followed by Turon.

This delicious sweetmeat appears in all the supermarkets in December. It is nougat flavoured with the almonds that grow so prolifically in Spain. I bought it in industrial quantities as it was so delicious. Christmas Day is usually spent quietly at home with the children receiving just one small present. Because the main present giving day is January 6th - Three kings day.

New Year's Eve in Spain is exciting with celebration on people's minds but it just happens later in the evening than most countries. We had been invited to the biggest party in the area and I was determined to attend. I bought a new dress and it was hanging in all its splendour in the wardrobe.

We had a lovely Christmas in England with the family and returned to Spain on December 31st. As we left London in the early morning it was starting to rain heavily but we did not notice it as we chattered away happily. We crossed the channel and realised it was starting to snow heavily. We had left plenty of time for our journey and so we were not worried about any delays.

That was until the traffic stopped on the Peripherique and there we stayed. The snow fell until we were in a complete whiteout and there was nothing we could do. We were fortunate as there was just the two of us and we had water and croissants so after playing a final desultory game of eye spy we both nodded off. The Scotch Wool Shop emergency but very itchy blanket just about covered both of us.
There we stayed until the radio rang out the midnight bells and we struggled to sit up the wish each other a Happy New Year. Our lips were too cold to attempt the regulatory kiss.

Not long after that a snow plough passed us and we were escorted with the next group of cars to the next motorway exit. We managed to get a room a very down market looking hotel but in our cold and dishevelled state we were grateful for anything. It was only as we were nodding off that I said plaintively "Oh no, we have missed the party!"

THE LOTUS GENERATION

We arrived back at our Spanish home to be regaled by all and sundry with details of the fabulous party and I had to sit and smile at all the appropriate junctures.

That evening I was doing that gormless thing of staring into the fridge that teenage boys do, when I spied a bunch of fat green grapes in the back of the fridge. I had bought these to celebrate New Year as the Spanish celebrate each chime of the bell with a grape for good luck in the coming year. I was too late to celebrate New Year but it was not too late for that huge piece of ripe Dolcelatte cheese that would go nicely with the grapes, thank you!

Kings Day Eve arrived and the weather was perfect for the anticipated parade. The Three Kings arrives by boat and the procession is amazing and awe inspiring. Camels and horses carry the Kings and their party aloft and the floats travelling behind are full of their helpers throwing thousands of sweets to the children and anyone else who is standing beside the road.

The sweets are hard caramelos and if you are unlucky enough to get one in the middle of the forehead a moment's dizziness ensues. The bright colours of the costumes and the music of the marching bands prove a heady mix and everyone is in good spirits as tomorrow is the day that the children receive their presents.

I got to wear my party dress that week as we had been invited to a masonic function by the friendly neighbour. The venue was up towards Valencia so we stayed in the hotel where the function was being held.

Just before we went down for the splendid dinner my sister Gillian and her husband called at our room for an aperitif. We toasted each other's health and as I looked at my sister I told her she looked stunning in her off the shoulder cream dress.

As the men left the room she sat down on the bed to refasten her four inch heels. The bed was very wide and as luck would have it she chose the exact spot where the beds met to perch her beautifully clad derriere. There was a loud scream as she fell through the gap in the beds and as her husband rushed to her rescue all we could see were her legs wiggling in the air. I tried hard not to laugh but eventually a faint murmur of hysteria escaped my lips and soon we were all laughing.

We managed to right her but she had been holding a glass of Cava as she fell, so a lot of dabbing and patting was in order before we could leave the room. All eyes were upon us as we made our way, with as much dignity as we could muster, to our seats. The evening was great fun and as the raffle was announced it turned out that we had won the first prize of a television.

The next morning we realised that the television would not go in the boot and so we girls had to sit with it on our knees all the way back home.

CHAPTER 57
Gilda From Guatemala

Blessed are the flexible for they shall not be bent out of shape.
Anon.

I worked with Gilda at the clinic on the coast about forty miles away from where we lived. She was a beautiful, wise woman from Guatemala and taught yoga in the sunshine. Gilda's husband Stein was a professor from Denmark and the last place they had lived was in Kenya.

We hit it off from the moment we were introduced and very soon she invited us to her home to have dinner. In England if someone invites you to dinner they usually give you two weeks' notice and if they say eight for eight thirty then you will probably be there at ten past the hour.

There were a few language difficulties until I understood that in Spain when you are invited by a Spanish person for dinner they mean that very night. We were invited for nine pm that evening. We got dressed up and were actually ringing the bell of her beautiful home at nine pm precisely. The roads had been clearer than I thought and we were there about ten minutes earlier than I had intended.

Nobody answered when we buzzed, all we could hear was a deep sonorous bark from inside the house. An elemental storm was beginning to brew over the sea. Grant sat down on the step and rested his head on a passing stone lion. "I think you have got this wrong, love. We are not expected here tonight."

I rang the bell one more time just to be sure and we had just turned to leave when the door opened. A pink bespectacled man opened the door and put his hand out "Please come in, you are very welcome, my name is Stein. As you know I am northern European so I will tell you that it took me a long time to learn. In Spain when they say come at nine that actually mean around about ten thirty!

He poured us a glass of something delicious and went to tell Gilda, who was in the bath, that she had guests. We chatted amongst ourselves whilst she got ready. There was a lovely old Labrador sitting by my chair. As I held my glass in my left hand I stroked his broad back with my right. I knew his name was Bruce as she had mentioned him to me.

When Gilda appeared in the doorway, looking fabulous she motioned us through to the dining room. As I stood up so did the Labrador and as he turned to face me I realised that he had miraculously turned into the biggest Rottweiler that I had ever seen. My heart did a summersault as I sidled past him to be seated for dinner. Stein said "We had him in Kenya and he guarded the compound, we did not have the heart to leave him behind when we moved to Spain"

We sat down at the brightly coloured table and I realised with a sinking heart that the first course was Gazpatcho. I had only had this at Home Counties dinner parties and I really did not care for the insipid liquid at any price. However, when I took a sip of this vegetable nectar that I was being served, near a Spanish beach, by a talented Guatemalan cook than I was converted for life.

I also met her daughter Mary that evening and was thoroughly entranced by her. Stunningly beautiful and fluent in seven languages she was a credit to her parents. Only in her mid-twenties she was already a cancer research scientist and martial arts expert. I think she was one of the most accomplished and delightful women I have ever met.

The journey home was eventful as the storm had settled in but we were full of bonhomie from our delightful hosts and decided to have them to us as soon as possible to hear more of their interesting lives.

CHAPTER 58
Get Me Off This Minute

It is not fair to ask of others what you are not willing to do yourself.
Eleanor Roosevelt

I was running training courses at that time and had found the best way to find lots of new clients was to go to the fairs that were held three or four times a year at local hotels in the area. There was always an eclectic mix of nationalities and interests and it was a good place to meet new people.

I always seemed to get lots of clients at this particular hotel and so I had a big stand and Grant helped me set up for the day. I was always dressed up for these occasions and this meant high heels of course. The stand on one side of me was doing permanent makeup and the other side was a famous local Spanish artist.

We watched fascinated as first one woman got eyebrows where she had not had them and the next one got her lips lined in a startling shade of pink. I was really unsure about the lipstick but the client seemed to like the result.

I was introduced to this woman formally at a dinner a few weeks later. I paid particular interest to her lips as the evening went on. I decided it was actually fine but wild horses would not make me had it done, as it looked too painful.

When my sister arrived for a look round my husband suggested that Gillian and I both went for some lunch. We had a look round at the fifty two stalls and then made our way down to the restaurant.

The ballroom where the fair was situated was on the second floor of the hotel and the restaurant was three floors down built into the side of the hill with views over the sea.

Spanish marble staircases look glorious but can be difficult to navigate especially in high heels. They swirl round in ever tighter circles which mean that at some points you have to let go of the banister you have been clutching for dear life, to make for a wider part of the step.

The alternative to this is to risk life and limb hanging on with tightly gripped hands with the added frisson of stepping into the abyss. All this and the steps are a slippery as any ice rink I have ever been on. The useful advice to any woman negotiating Spanish stairs has to be "one need ones full concentration". Gillian and I had completely forgotten this advice in our determination to exchange information as we had not seen each other since, well since eight am that morning!

She stepped out first, tip toeing as delicately as she could but getting into her stride as we rounded the first bend. She looked lovely in a black Spanish style dress with a tight fitting skirt. I followed in a Max Mara suit with a cream blouse that buttoned up the front.

I could hear a conversation going on behind me and had just registered that it was in German when Gillian let out the most terrible scream and disappeared shouting "Oh bloody hell!"

She is my little sister, what could I do? I tried to grab her, missed and fell down after her. That terrible feeling when you know you are falling, hit my solar plexus and I screamed. I do not know what I screamed as I was too busy falling to listen. I would venture it was a lot worse than "Oh, bloody hell."

When the kind German lady behind me tried to stem my fall she joined us hurtling down the stairs shouting whatever the German equivalent is of "Oh bloody hell."

Her husband must have made a rather half-hearted, in my view, attempt to grab her as he managed to stay upright. We landed with such a clatter that people came running from all directions. I looked up to find a cheery chap with his hand on my chest saying laughingly "Do not worry dear I am a doctor."

I struggled to my feet and brushed him away "You cheeky monkey I have just seen you manning the handmade soap stand"

We all managed to get up right without too much injury other than to pride. I did not feel too bad about the slightly twisted elbow I sustained as I had nine new clients for my course that started two weeks after the multinational slippery stair incident.

CHAPTER 59
The Oldest Restaurant In The World

One cannot think well, love well, sleep well if one has not dined well.
Virginia Wolfe

Gillian, Malcolm, Grant and I decided to go to Madrid one weekend and set off on the trip in good spirits. My brother-in-law Malcolm had booked the reservation and he is known for his attachment to economy above everything else and you were never sure what you would get with him. We discovered with relief that our hotel was very central and we could walk to most places.

The first evening we had reservations at Sobrino de Botin which was famous as the oldest restaurant in the world. We squeezed into our seats as the place is small and built into what looks like a cave. I had done my research and discovered that the restaurant had opened in 1725 and had been mentioned in Ernest Hemingway's novel *The Sun Also Rises*. The painter Francisco de Goya had worked there whilst waiting to take up his place at the Royal academy of Fine Arts.

The most famous dishes on the menu were Sopa de Ajo (an egg in chicken broth) and Conchinillo Asado (Roast Suckling Pig). I was lost in a reverie watching Madrid's elegant intelligentsia chatting away whilst tucking into suckling pig. Frankly it did not look easy to my untrained eye, within a moment I turned around to find a dish of steaming broth at my elbow. Well, to be frank it looked like a dish of boiling water with an insipid, spread-eagled egg floating in it.

I smiled my thanks at the young waiter and picked up my spoon. Anyone who knows me knows I only have one egg a year and I was not going to waste it on this dish. I stirred it around and when no one was looking pushed the dish surreptitiously away from me.

The suckling pig fared better but I found it difficult to navigate and after finishing our wine and coffee we were out on the street. Two minutes later my sister stopped and said in an alarmed voice "I have left my new Jonathan Saunders jacket in there" and turned on her heel and ran.

Well, I say ran but as she had on four inch heels and a straight skirt so it was more of a hobble on the cobbles. Her husband passed her easily and was back at the restaurant in a flash. His mastery of the language was almost perfect, so a search was soon instigated but to no avail, it appeared the said jacket was missing. My sister carried on a bit but eventually we had to accept the inevitable and we repaired into a nearby Mexican bar. "Oh I am so cross," muttered my sister, "I do not know what to do" as she downed her first tequila.

We had such fun that night in that little piece of Mexico, singing, dancing, margaritas and as much chilli and burritos as we could eat.

The oldest restaurant in the world became known as "The Case of the Disappearing Jacket place" in their house.

CHAPTER 60
The Railroad Station

That life quickening atmosphere of a big railway station where everything is something trembling on the brink of something else.
Vladimir Nabokov

The next morning we set off for Atocha Railroad Station. The main hall is a tropical greenhouse full of amazing plants. The atrium and garden full of over seven thousand plants are mostly tropical and we spent a contented hour wandering round.

Then the business of the day began and the chaps went one way and the girls went the other. Shopping at the gallerias was why we were there as Gillian was determined to replace her jacket and buy shoes. Spanish women's shoes are just perfect stylish, exquisite, soft leather and comfortable even when the heels are as high as the sky. I loved them to distraction and when I found a pair in my size I fell on them like manna from heaven. The trouble was my feet are very large whereas my sister has elegant feet four sizes smaller. The whole panoply of Spanish women's shoes was available for her perusal and peruse she did for what seemed like a very long time.

I got so bored and distracted at one point that I wandered into the boutique next door. I wondered up and down, not really expecting to find something in my size. Then, there it was, the most beautiful green suede jacket I had ever seen. A shade somewhere between fern and moss with a sheepskin lining it drew me across the room.

My hand reached out unbidden to touch the butter soft garment as the assistant floated across the room. In one fell swoop the jacket was on my back, smiled at in approval and wrapped carefully in matching tissue paper. I handed her my card without giving a fig for the cost and was out of the shop carrying a very stylish pink carrier bag.

I walked back into the shoe store to see my distracted sister staring at herself in a long mirror. "What do you think?" she said. I stared at the two odd shoes "I prefer the one on the left" I replied. "You know I think I will have both pairs, as they both fit" she murmured.

She put one of her boots back on and then followed the assistant to the till holding the other boot in her hand. I followed her as if we were in some crazy one legged race and realised with chagrin that she had not noticed that I had been gone.

CHAPTER 61
Our Visit To The Prado

Not all those who wander are lost.
J.R. Tolkien

We had time to visit the beautiful park before our trip to the museum. We stopped at the statue of Don Quixote. We could not read the brass sign as it was too high up. Malcolm said "This is Don Quixote and his faithful servant Pancho Sanchez. They went around tilting at windmills."

Grant replied "Well actually I know about something about tilting at windmills but I think you will find his servant was called Sancho Panchez".

With that he walked off and Gillian and I followed him. We looked back to see Malcolm on his tip toes trying to read the inscription before he caught site of us laughing and realised that Grant was just having some fun with him.

THE LOTUS GENERATION

Whenever we visit a gallery that we had not been to before, we always try to hire a guide to show us things that we would never find out by just looking round.

Our elegant Madrilenian guide Valentina was waiting for us on the steps of the Prado. This visit was the real reason we had come to Madrid and I was hoping to make the most of the afternoon. We spent a wonderful informative afternoon studying the works of Francesco de Goya, Diego Valazquez, and Bartolome Esteban Murillo as well as Picasso and Dali. We agreed to meet up in the café for a coffee when we had finished wandering around.

Gillian, Grant and I were waiting for ages and it seemed Malcolm had disappeared. My sister suddenly lifted her arm in the air and yelling "Hieronymus Bosch!" ran off.

Whatever it was it sounded serious and so we followed her down two flights of stairs and there was Malcolm staring mesmerised at a painting. He loved this Dutch painter from the renaissance era and whilst they stood chatting about it, I went to the museum shop to buy him a copy of "The Garden of Earthly Delights" as a thank you for organising the trip.

I got the assistant to put it in a large bag as I actually found the moral and religious imagery a bit scary and did not want to look too hard at all the poor figures.

We had a wonderful walk round the centre that evening and then ate tapas to finish our short trip and the thing we all agreed on was that we would come back soon.

CHAPTER 62
The Road To Granada

If you do not know where you are going, any road will get there.
Lewis Carroll

I was thinking to myself "How lucky I was to be here in this place." I was sitting in the car with my husband on a perfect sunny day, feeling peaceful, happy and relaxed on the road to Granada.

THE LOTUS GENERATION

I felt my eyelids droop and then drift slowly closed. I relaxed completely when I felt the first rays of sunlight on my face. Soon the miles were rolling by and I had never felt so calm and peaceful in my life.

I shifted in my seat and wound down the window to breathe in the crisp mountain air. I felt as though I had been in the Sierra Nevada forever as the perfect azure blue sky pierced my closed lids. I forced opened my eyes and saw the road signs for magical cities like Seville, Cordoba and Cadiz calling to us as we passed.

The road seemed to be going on and on in a shimmering haze. Gnarled, ancient olive trees stretched as far as the eye could see with their precious crop glinting in the sunlight. Then with another breath, the scent of lemons was everywhere.

Then the cool raindrops misted my face as a raincloud passed overhead. Soon it was gone and the lemon scent was intensified all around us. "Wow, what's that fabulous smell" said my husband as he took a deep slow breath. We had hardly spoken in the two hours we had been travelling as we were both enjoying the Spanish classical guitar concert on the radio. "Lemons" I whispered without opening my eyes.

A half an hour went by and then Grant said "open your eyes and look at the navy mountains in the distance, they look stunning with their fluffy topping of white clouds".

I looked around as the music changed key and a whole new picture came into view. The well-travelled road to Granada with its white houses and red roofs sparkled in the distance.

The Alhambra Palace soon came into view and we marvelled at such a thing of beauty built so many centuries ago.

We parked the car and began to walk along the cobbled path surrounded by a beautiful garden. We were mesmerised and peeping over the wall we could see Granada in all its glory down below. The perfume of the roses in the palace garden was stunning, filling your senses like a magical mist and somehow brought you closer to the history of this medieval palace. Various shades of pink, white, yellow and cream roses surrounded by perfect lines of scented lavender stretched your eyes out into eternity.

The large oak door blocked our path and then we were summoned through by an old curator. A cool marble entrance and a thousand twinkling stars above and I knew I would always remember this place in my heart.

Then Grant whispered "I have just seen a smart restaurant through a chink in the door, are you hungry? I nodded and soon we were seated in the most divine space next to a tinkling stream full of darting silver and golden fishes. I do not remember ordering anything but delicious dishes arrived and were replaced by even tastier ones until finally iced lemon Granizados and coffee arrived to complete our meal.

It was the cool of the evening when we left to find our car and all the visitors seemed to have disappeared into the mist. Grant and I had hardly spoken for hours but we had spent one of the most perfect days we had ever had.

CHAPTER 63
Ambrosia From The Indoor Barbecue

A good traveller is not intent on arriving.
Chinese proverb

When we found our hotel it was just perfect and after we dropped our bags we went for a walk. We stopped to drink red wine in the local bar and although we said we were not hungry the tapas was too tempting to refuse.

We shared tiny dishes of salty anchovies, fat green olives and hot, paprika scented chorizo with fried patatas. We walked back up the hill in the moonlight to our small hotel and shared a brandy with the owner before falling into a deep dreamless sleep.

The next morning, our journey home was to take us through some of the scenic Spanish countryside that we had not visited before. As we skirted the floor of the mountains the air went much colder and we could see snow on the tops of the Sierra Nevada Mountains.

The scenery was breath-taking and we marvelled at the picture perfect villages as we passed them. Bougainvillea was everywhere in shades of pink, lilac and deep red against the traditional, white villas that sparkled in the midday sun.

Little old ladies were sitting dressed in black on their porches peeling ripe, juicy tomatoes and pungent purple garlic for the family lunch whilst their husbands were perched on stools outside the village bar consuming copious quantities red wine or brandy. We waved and they acknowledged us with a nod as we passed.

Around two pm we were starting to get hungry and Grant decided, "we are going to stop at the next place whatever it is." I muttered darkly, "On you own head be it!" as I knew his philosophy either resulted in delight or disaster.

Eventually we pulled up outside what could only be described as a large square roadside hacienda or Venta, a family run restaurant. We parked outside amongst cars, pickup trucks and Lorries. We walked through the archway and when our eyes were accustomed to the gloom an amazing sight awaited us. Dark, rough-hewn chairs and tables in their hundreds were set all around the biggest indoor wood burning fire we had ever seen.

The flames reached up into the open sky and cuts of lamb, beef and pork of every description were being thrown in to the flames. About a dozen women were running around taking orders and sitting at the bar we decided on lamb chops. To say they were ambrosia would be to understate the deliciousness of our lunch that day. We spent two happy hours with the locals enjoying great company.

Interestingly we have tried several times to revisit that place but could never find it again.

I often wonder if we dreamt a shimmering mirage that perfect sunny day.

CHAPTER 64
Our Son Is Getting Married

It is sometimes essential for a man and wife to quarrel: they get to know each other better that way.

Goethe

This was to be one of our happiest of days. Our youngest son James was getting married and we were so excited. His brother Theo was to be his best man as James had stood for him a decade before.

THE LOTUS GENERATION

When Theo was married his brother was still at University and was only nineteen years old. Now James was getting married and Theo was just about to become a father for the second time.

Theo's wife was due to have a baby girl four weeks after the wedding and she and I went to the hairdressers together. We carried our fascinators carefully, each perfectly tissue wrapped in a smart hat box. Suzanne's hat was cream and a mix of tall feathers and leaves to match her cream flowing dress. My fascinator was the palest of pink with seed pearls and a tiny net covering. It was the exact same colour as my Paule Vasseur silk suit. Suzanne could only just climb into the chair to have her hair done and I sat patiently whilst my long hair was wound into a perfect chignon.

We left the hairdressers later than we had intended and went to get in her car. She was a tall, elegant young woman but with her hat attached firmly to her head she was well over six feet tall. I tried every way to get my heavily pregnant daughter-in-law into the car whilst we were both laughing so much at the absurdity of the situation.

We could not undo the fascinator as it was clipped so firmly in place. Eventually she lay across the back seat of the car as I drove very carefully the five miles back to the hotel where we were all staying.

James had so many friends and they were all there that perfect sunny day. His friends from school, university and rugby all smartly dressed in morning suits and in great spirits. After university many of his friends had moved to America and Australia but they had all come back for his wedding.

The sun shone that perfect August day and there was a sense of delicious anticipation in the air. I was standing on the grand staircase of the hotel where we were all staying watching Alistair my talented photographer son-in-law taking his marvellous shots.

Out of the corner of my eye I saw the bride's mother Peggy staggering under the weight of a four tier wedding cake. I assumed it was her as I could only see her legs and feet as the rest of her was covered by white icing and pink rosebuds.

I stood up to go and help her when I saw her husband, who had been parking the car, rushing to her aid.

THE LOTUS GENERATION

"Too late," was the cry as she overbalanced and so unfortunately did the wedding cake that had been made so lovingly by a family friend.

Peggy stood with her arms in the air and her mouth in a perfect O, as if she could not believe her eyes.

The hotel staff rushed forwards and it was soon scooped up and removed. The cake was there for the cutting ceremony but I noticed nobody was offered a piece with the coffee. Soon all the guests arrived and we were so delighted to see them all.

An hour later we were all ready and seated, waiting for the start of the proceedings. This was my youngest son's wedding and I was feeling a little nervous so held on to Grant's hand tightly.

As the start of the wedding music sounded and we got to our feet, the darling bridesmaids made their appearance. One by one in their delightful matching dresses they walked down the aisle holding there bouquets of fragrant lilac freesias and then the two year old pageboy Felix followed. He was not quite sure about his pale grey suit, and walked diffidently behind them.

Everyone gasped as James' beautiful bride Emma walked towards us with her proud father. She looked stunning, that wonderful day in her enchanting gown covered in delicate seed pearls with a long flowing train. She wore her long blonde hair pinned up with flowers framing her lovely face and carried long stemmed lilies and white roses in her arms.

They looked so in love as they caught sight of each other and held hands as their vows were exchanged. I felt that thrill of emotion that a mother feels when she knows her precious child is marrying the right person. This was my third and last child to be married and I was enjoying every minute of it.

It fell to my daughter Miranda to do the reading of the Shakespeare sonnet no 116, whilst clutching her smallest child in her arms. Every family wedding in recent times had included this sonnet.

> Let me not to the marriage of true minds.
> Admit impediments. Love is not love
> Which alters when it alteration finds,
> Or bends with the remover to remove;
> Oh no! It is an ever-fixed mark

THE LOTUS GENERATION

>That looks on tempests and is never shaken;
>It is the star to every wandering bark,
>Whose worth's unknown, although his height be taken,
>Loves not times fool, through rosy lips and cheeks
>Within his bending sickles compass come:
>Love alters not within brief hours and weeks,
>But bears it out even to the edge of doom.
>If this be error and upon me proved,
>I never writ, nor no man ever loved.

The wedding breakfast was delicious and the speeches funny and memorable. The bride's father, John had played the saxophone in a dance band for many years and treated us to an hour of wonderful music with his band.

Then the real fun began with began with a DJ and everyone got up and danced until dawn. Everyone danced that is, except Grant and I who rounded all the grandchildren up and headed for bed.

The happy couple left next morning for three weeks in Italy starting with a leisurely drive down the Amalfi coast road.

CHAPTER 65
I Love Going To Barcelona

>Always do sober what you said you would do drunk. That will teach you to keep your mouth shut.
>
>*Ernest Hemingway*

I love Barcelona as there is always something new to discover. We visited the city about eight times whilst we were living in Spain.

Our first visit included a trip to La Sagrada Familia. This large Roman Catholic unfinished Basilica was designed by Catalan architect Antoni Gaudi. The building was started in 1882 and is not expected to be finished until 2041. Gaudi spent the last 15 years of his life working exclusively on the project and it is like nothing else you have ever seen. There is not one straight line anywhere in the building and it was inspired by the curves and flow of nature.

The columns supporting the inside of the church look like trees and their branches support the roof with mathematical precision. After

THE LOTUS GENERATION

we had finished our tour we stood for a long time on the pavement staring up at the edifice trying to commit its beauty to our memory banks.

We visited the Picasso museum one rainy afternoon and we expected to enjoy the cultural experience as we usually did. We were both very quiet when we came out on that particularly grey afternoon. As we sat enjoying a cortado and restorative brandy we mulled over this unusual reaction.

The museum has an exhaustive collection from Picasso's blue period. This is the period between 1900 and 1904 when he painted monochrome paintings in shades of blue and green. These works appear to be very sombre and are said to reflect his experience of poverty and instability: the characters are beggars, street urchins, prostitutes, the blind and drunks. We decided that the exquisite drawings had been meant to have exactly that unedifying effect on us and so his paintings from that period had done their job.

A walk down Las Ramblas is not to be missed. A tree lined pedestrian mall whose crowds add to the magic of the area. Along the promenade's length are flower sellers who display the most exquisite flowers from every colour palate of the rainbow.

Birds in even more amazing shades swoop and trill tunefully from their many cages hanging from the trees. There are street traders selling everything the heart desires, whatever kind of restaurants you fancy, street performers and bars for the ubiquitous tapas and whatever drink will quench your thirst. A more cosmopolitan walk down to the sea you will not find anywhere in the world

Most of our visits to Barcelona were to do with my work as I was involved in teaching NLP in Spain. On our final visit we stayed in the most interesting hotel that had been a museum in a previous incarnation. We stayed there for a week and never saw another soul which felt frankly strange.

The reason for this visit was to see something called the Heroes Journey by Stephen Gilligan and Robert Dilts. It is about a journey of self-discovery and it is based on the work of Joseph Campbell who had lived most of his life in Hawaii.

I had always been fascinated with the work of Joseph Campbell. He was an American mythologist, writer and lecturer best known for his work in comparative religion and comparative mythology. His philosophy was "Follow your Bliss."

George Lucas credited Campbell's Heroes Journey as an influence on the Star Wars film. My favourite quote of Joseph Campbell's is ......

"Each entered the forest at a point that he himself had chosen where it was darkest and there was no path. If there is a path it is someone else's path and you are not on an adventure."

The Heroes Journey Seminar was in English with subsequent translation into Spanish. As I looked around the room at several hundred young Spanish people I realised that to a man they had no need of the translation. I realised then that the world was becoming a smaller place each day.

I enjoyed the story of the journey and made up my mind to put a visit to Hawaii to the top of my bucket list.

CHAPTER 66
Your Bucket List Has Arrived Madam

One does not discover new lands without consenting to lose sight of the shore for a long time.

Andre Gide

About a month after we got back from Barcelona I was looking on the internet and found the most wonderful trip. Grant was away for a couple of days so I had to take a risk if I booked it without talking to him first.

I did what I always did when I had a problem and lifted my eyes up from my desk and stared at the imposing Montgo Mountain. As usual the top was shrouded in mist and today there was no inspiration available for me.

I walked into the kitchen and looked at the clock on the wall six pm. It was time for a glass of chilled white wine as the sun was over the yard arm somewhere in the world. I wandered out onto the terrace and stared across at the view.

If I stared to my right I could see the sea sparkling and rolling in to the shore and bathed in the evening sunset. If I looked ahead I could see thousands upon thousands of green leaved trees studied with perfect orange globes with a back drop of deepest tangerine. This orb was the setting sun looking like a fireball in the clear western sky. My eyes moved left and the Spanish villas with a *mise en scène* of navy mountains held my gaze and also my thoughts.

I sat for a while with more on my mind than in it. Then suddenly I jumped up and rushed back into my office and with a flourish pressed the button. Two weeks holiday in the States with our final destination of Hawaii.

The next day as I cleared my diary I hoped Grant would be as excited with my impetuous act as I was. I looked out of the window and waited for the sight of his red Alpha Romeo coming back down the road back from his trip to Madrid. I had cooked his favourite dish of fish soup for his supper and hoped that would sway the deal.

PART THREE

CHAPTER 67
The Man With Blue Shoes

A traveller without observation is a bird without wings.
Moslih Eddin Saadi

"Is your wife with you?" the machine was asking my perplexed husband. We were at Heathrow airport preparing to board a United Airlines Boeing 767 to Chicago and we were checking in without benefit of human interaction. Grant pressed "Yes" and then the next question was "Would you like to upgrade for the entire seven flights that you are about to embark on?" The dollar amount mentioned was so reasonable that he pressed "Yes" before we could discuss it. "Okay with me," I thought as we moved on to the next step of our journey.

And so began the most amazing two weeks of my whole life. We flew in wonderful comfort to Chicago and had to wait four hours for our plane to San Francisco. We wandered around the airport and I did what I always do, I ended up in a bookshop.

THE LOTUS GENERATION

There was a guy there in his thirties who was so excited to be on his first book signing tour and we started up a conversation. He was so proud of his book which was a mystery set in the time of the Pharaohs and of course I bought a copy and he signed it for me.

I had decided some years before that I was going to offer a questioning and pleasant demeanour to the outside world whenever I travelled. I postulate the theory that if you are interested in people they will return the favour and you will discover things that you could only dream of.

The bonus is in this amazing time of social media you can keep up with everybody you ever meet.

Our flight was called and we set off to find the gate for our onward journey. The cabin stewards came around with boxes of food and we could not believe our eyes. Here were the two oldest people I had ever seen.

The man looked like Aloysius Parker, Lady Penelope's butler from the Thunderbirds TV series. He could only walk if he was propped up by the food trolley. His wife, Hilda, for he introduced her to us, looked like the old lady in the 1955 black comedy *The Lady Killers* with Alec Guinness.

I was thinking about this gallant old couple who would probably never see eighty again still working and 50,000 feet in the air at that. That must have been my last thought as I woke up as we were coming in to land at San Francisco International Airport. We decided we did not need a car and so we hopped into a taxi.

After lunch we decided to go for a walk and just enjoy the air. We both love this place and always tried to make the most of the visit. We walked up hill and down again and eventually came across the fascinating Episcopal Grace Cathedral on Nob Hill. We walked up the steps and almost bumped into a man going in the opposite direction. We introduced ourselves and he turned out to be a native of Edinburgh who had lived and worked at the Cathedral for more than twenty five years. He put aside his journey and offered to show us round this centre for international pilgrimage.

The stained glass windows, which are my particular interest, were stunning and the mosaics were by Jan Henryk de Rosen, a famous Polish artist. We loved the international and welcoming feel of this hallowed space and gave our heartfelt thanks to William our Scottish guide.

We had our usual supper on Fisherman's Wharf and headed back to our hotel for an early night.

The next morning after eggs over easy and a stack of pancakes with maple syrup we headed over to Union Square. We both had things to do and so agreed to meet for lunch at the Cheesecake Factory on the eighth floor of the Macy building.

I needed some shoes for a wedding and as I had already bought a new handbag in London I knew the exact shade of palatinate royal blue that I wanted.

I wandered into Saks Fifth Avenue store in Union Square and so began my search in earnest. I started at the top floor knowing full well that the shoes were on the ground floor. Two hours later armed with a beautiful piece of turquoise jewellery and a new Anya Hindmarsh makeup bag I finally reached terra firma.

I looked at every pair of blue high heeled shoes they had for sale in that store but nothing came close to my dream colour. I sighed with resignation and made for the Union Square exit.

As I glanced down to be sure of my footing I realised with a start that I was looking at a pair of shoes in exactly the right shade of blue, only the problem was that they were attached to somebody else's feet. An invisible, unbroken thread drew me through the crowds and across the pavement unbidden.

There the owner of the magic royal blue shoes stood at least six foot four inches tall and his bearing was that of a soldier. His shoes matched his royal blue three piece suit and royal blue bowler hat. Even though this elegant, silver haired African American man must have been in his eighties, his beautiful voice was as clear as a bell.

I put some money in his coffer and stood leaning on the brick wall, entranced and listening to him croon a medley of tuneful songs that were all somewhere in my musical memory.

Eventually we were alone and as he removed his blue bowler hat he asked "Where are you from Ma'am?"

"I am from London" I replied."

"Well now, I have been there and have met the Queen "he said.

THE LOTUS GENERATION

I smiled and he went on "I used to sing with the Doo Wop[1] group The Inkspots and we were invited to sing at the Royal Variety Performance. It was a wonderful day."

He went on to tell me his life story and we were a good way through before he excused himself to sing to the gathering crowds again.

Just before he left me he reached in his pocket and pulled out a postcard with his picture on the front in his blue suit. He told me the name of the artist that had painted it and wrote her phone number on the back of the postcard.

I stood still for a moment thinking this was perfectly serendipitous as one of the reasons I had made this trip was the thought of adding an online art gallery to my business. I was actually looking for American Artists to add to the European ones we already had.

I realised the time and then rushed across the square and up to the Cheesecake Factory to meet my husband. Grant had already found us a table on the roof terrace overlooking Union Square and there was a welcoming chilled martini with a tart green olive waiting for me. After rushing around for so long I was just happy to sit and relax in the warm sunshine.

We ordered Caesar salads as we were eating out that night. We could not leave without sampling the cheesecake and plumped for a shared piece of blueberry cheesecake before wandering back to the hotel.

As we were heading back I remembered the list of jeans to buy that I had been given by my daughter. We stood in the gloomy store on the phone with her whilst she gave me the measurements. The staff were very helpful and I left with everything she wanted.

The next day I rang the phone number on the card and then drove out to Point Reyes to meet the artist and look at her colourful paintings. After spending a lovely morning with her she agreed that I

---

[1] Doo Wop is a style of vocal based rhythm and blues music popular with African American communities in the 1940s and it went on to have main stream popularity in the 1950s and 1960s .

could show her work on my online gallery. A successful visit all round.

CHAPTER 68
How Long Does It Take To Get To Hawaii?

We live in a wonderful world that is full of beauty, charm and adventure. There is no end to adventures if only we seek them with our eyes open.

Nehru

In my fevered imagination Hawaii was a tiny, glittering Island just off the west coast of The States. The reality of course is very different and as we waved goodbye to San Francisco and settled in for a five hour flight I began to read up on our destination.

"Hawaii is the only US state made up of islands and it is the most northern island in Polynesia...."

I closed my eyes whilst visualising warm, tropical beaches. I dreamed of Tom Selleck waiting at the airport to greet me with flowered lei to place around my neck. In my dream I could dance the Hula and as I was swivelling my hips the plane landed with a bump and I was back to reality in this magical place.

Dark grey clouds greeted us and I pulled my pink Escada jacket a little tighter as the wind whistled around us whilst we were waiting for a taxi. Our driver was a delightful woman named Alana who was more than happy to tell us the story of the native people on our journey to the hotel. She told us about the history of the Islands and the schools and the language as she drove us past the University.

I was interested to learn about the alphabet as all the words seemed to be made up of similar sounds, vowels A,E,I,O,U and consonants H,K,L,M,N,P and W.

I did not have time to ask any more questions as she stopped with a flourish outside our hotel. The whole place was surrounded by gardens full of the national flowers of Hawaii, Pua Aloalo or the yellow hibiscus.

We registered at reception and were taken up to the room. Grant was not very impressed but the views from the large windows made up for the rather 1970s decoration.

THE LOTUS GENERATION

A small snooze was in order and when we woke up the sun was out again and a hazy light covered everything. Grant went off to hire a car and I could not resist the lure of the sumptuous garden.

We were on the Island of Oahu in the capital city of Honolulu where their national flower yellow Ilima is used to make the famous neck garlands or leis. When I held the flower gently in my hand I realised it was a tiny version of the ubiquitous hibiscus. As I examined it, I ran my thumb over it delicate fuzzy petals. I heard a very faint snap and there it was, sitting in the palm of my hand. The elderly gardener who was standing not far away smiled and signalled to me to tuck it in my hair. I fiddled about a bit and then voila, I was suddenly an Island girl.

The gardener insisted in showing me round the hotel grounds. Discussion was not a problem for us, as English is also an official language. The stunning red flowers that I was drawn to were in fact Lehua blossoms, from the native Ohia tree. This flower is sacred to Pele, Hawaii's volcanic goddess.

I was having a lovely time and was completely absorbed when a head I recognised popped up over the hedge and nodding towards the open road said "Fancy a spin, gorgeous?"

Within three hours of arriving in Oahu I was rolling along the coast road in an open topped white Ford Mustang with a flower in my hair. My Hawaiian adventure had begun and I was going to enjoy every minute of it.

CHAPTER 69
Our Little Wander

There are no foreign lands. It is the traveller only who is foreign.
Robert Louis Stephenson

Our hotel was two minutes' walk from Waikiki beach and there were promising looking restaurants all around the hotel. We settled on salads and cold beers that night and as we chatted I remarked that I had not seen many shops in the area. "Can we please have a little wander before we go back to the hotel?" I asked.

Pleasantly replete, we headed for the beach front hand in hand. As we turned a corner we could not believe our eyes. Tasteful, bright neon lights shone brightly from every available space. Here in Honolulu were higher end department stores than I have ever seen in any one place including New York and London.

Every passer-by was carrying a panoply of exquisite carrier bags in shades of every imaginable colour. Young women and men had been shopping in Chanel, Prada, Gucci, Louis Vuitton, Vivienne Westwood and Hermes to name a few. They had their prized possessions on show to the world.

We headed for the nearest hostelry to recover our powers of speech and sat down with a lovely American couple. The first thing he said, "We come here every year to get away from the cold Missouri winters" The first thing she said was "I have never met any English people here before. We have seen lots of Americans, Australians, Canadians and Japanese but not many Europeans at all."

Then together they said "Tonight is Lindy Hoppers night upstairs, why don't you come with us?" The lessons we had taken in Spain had paid off after all and we were able to dance along to the swing band with abandon. Our first day and night in Honolulu had been magical. We staggered on our tired feet back to bed, full of cocktails and bonhomie, in that order.

The next morning we went gift shopping. Colourful Hawaiian shirts for sons and grandsons were *de rigueur*. Hawaiian dresses for the granddaughters and jewellery for the daughters were soon purchased. Then we bought macadamia nuts in tins, in chocolate and any one of the thousand ways that they are available there.

We had fun that morning buying things that would probably never be worn. We were in a carefree mood as we stopped for lunch before embarking on our afternoon trip.

We were headed for Diamond Head beach where generations of surfers of all ages have ridden the waves. The beach that sparkles so dramatically in the overhead sun is located at the foothills of an extinct volcano at the eastern end of Waikiki .The beach is narrow and I would not want to swim there but I pulled my macadamia nut sun lotion from my hibiscus strewn orange beach bag and closed my eyes. Two seconds later as I was applying sun tan lotion by touch rather than sight when a shadow fell across my path. "I am not that keen on it here, should be go for a drive?"

THE LOTUS GENERATION

I staggered to my feet pushing everything back into my beach bag. Whilst I was walking back across the beach I realised that gritty, painful sand was stuck to all the little places that I had just applied sun tan lotion to so assiduously.

CHAPTER 70
Three Tiny White Horses

Life is all rainbows and unicorns.
Anon.

We actually had a delightful afternoon. Driving around that bucolic scene was a perfect pleasure. We saw mile after mile of fruit farms with pineapples, papayas and melons mounded up on carts for passers-by to purchase for a few cents in the honesty box.

We stopped at Pearl Harbour to stand and think for a moment about the two and a half thousand people that had died and the fact that the surprise attack here had caused the Americans to enter the Second World War. The hostilities by the Japanese lasted less than two hours but changed the course of history.

We set off again but with our mood chastened we decided to stop for a cooling drink. The place we chose was more like a shack than a café but I was taken by the tiny white horses in the garden. As we sat down the friendly proprietor brought us a jug of refreshing lemonade and discovering that we were hungry we ordered a sandwich. She brought us her speciality which was copious amounts of sweet pulled pork between large slabs of local bread. The food smelled delicious and caught the attention of the three tiny horses. As they walked towards me I thought that they looked more like unicorns when I shielded my eyes in the sunshine.

One by one they put their heads through the window, or where the window had once been, and they seemed to be asking for a bite of our sandwiches. We looked back at our host for instruction.

The lovely Hawaiian lady's feet glided across the tiled floor in her worn, straw sandals and she placed a dish full of tiny red apples

THE LOTUS GENERATION

on our table. Then she asked us to give Snowy, Pearl and Diamond one of the apples instead of bread.

Within two minutes of eating we were surrounded by birds including a pink parrot and two white toy poodles.

I felt like Dr Doolittle that afternoon as I found myself talking to all the animals.

CHAPTER 71
The Valley Of The Temples

Look at the stars lighting up the sky, no one of them stays in the same place.
Lucius Annaeus Seneca

As a very spiritual person I was drawn by an invisible thread to the place we visited the next morning.

It was raining and the mist hung like shadowy wraiths around the mountain tops. The hood was down on the mustang even though it was raining. The precipitation felt soft, it was of the dewy variety where the raindrops coat your hair with a sparkling hairnet of diamonds and it makes your skin feel like velvet. We tuned in to a local radio station and our favourite song was He'eia, about surfing and the King. A one hour pleasant drive and our destination appeared like a mirage before us.

At the foot of the Ko'olau Mountains in Valley of the Temples Memorial Park is the exquisite and breath taking Byodo-in Buddhist Temple.

The Temple in O'ahu is an exact, but smaller replica of the 950 year old Byodo –in Temple which is a United Nations World Heritage Centre in Uju, Japan.

The garden is a paradise that has been artfully landscaped to blend with the surrounding mountains and about the grounds you can see wild peacocks strutting and preening. We were fortunate and spied a majestic creature with its tail fanned out in various shades of blue, green and brown. It had a hundred black round eyes seeming to stare sightlessly in our direction.

The Japanese maple trees covered the gardens with their red, green, purple and brown leaves and were planted as far as the eye could see.

THE LOTUS GENERATION

This Byodo-in Temple welcomes people of all faiths or none to meditate pray or simply absorb the atmosphere of these beautiful grounds. The sound of the Buddhist Monks chiming the bells struck a chord deep in my chest and we went straight in to the Temple for a period of reflection.

The Temple was built in the 1960s to commemorate the hundredth anniversary of the arrival of the first Japanese immigrants to work in the sugar plantation fields.

The first person I saw when I finished meditating and stepped out into the sunlight was a Japanese lady artist who was painting tiny cards and book marks on her easel. I went to speak to her and bought some of her pictures that she wrapped artfully in tissue and raffia. We exchanged addresses and we went on to show her paintings on our online gallery.

We spent a further hour in the grounds searching out the water features. There were large reflecting ponds full of silver and gold shimmering koi carp and perches near tinkling waterfalls where you could enjoy the view.

As we were leaving we stopped to look at the notice board and read that the gardens had appeared in episodes of Magnum, Lost and Hawaii Five O and I was not a bit surprised.

Drat, I thought, I have missed Tom Selleck again!

CHAPTER 72
The Last Day At Luau

Kipa hou mai..Come visit again.

Our last day in Hawaii was spent at a Luau. We had been invited to this family party by our lovely driver Alana.

A Luau is a feast or party accompanied by entertainment. As you passed the beach at weekend you can see tents erected in the sand and people having a wonderful time.

The Luau is not just a party for the local people; it is part of the Hawaiian culture going back centuries. Until the nineteenth century the men and women ate separately. This custom was abolished by

THE LOTUS GENERATION

King Kamehameha 11 who officially ended the religious tradition by eating with the women. The King died from the measles in England in 1824.

As we walked across the hot sand at Waikiki beach we could smell the delicious barbequed meat and fish. Everyone was very friendly and made us feel welcome on that delightful afternoon.

The first dish I was offered was chicken baked in coconut milk, then a delicious salmon dish with something called taro that I had never tasted before. The cool refreshing beer was delicious.

This was a lei party and everyone made their own from the piles of brightly coloured flowers and beads that were laid out along long tables. I looked around and discovered that the women wore flowers around their neck and the men wore the beads.

When we were all replete the music and dancing started. Most of the men played the ukulele and the music was exquisite. For a fleeting moment I thought about George Formby and wondered how two such different sounds could come out of the same instrument!

The drummers sounded out a beat in time to the ukulele and soon the whole beach was up on their bare feet and dancing. As the sun started to set in the west we thanked our hosts and tip-toed away to begin our last drive in the mustang.

We were leaving this enchanting place to fly back to Los Angeles and then on to Las Vegas for a few days.

CHAPTER 73
Would You Move Us From This Table?

You are not drunk if you can lie on the floor without holding on.
Dean Martin

Waiting by the doors I was feeling somewhat perturbed. I did not like lifts at the best of times and I knew I had to whizz many storeys into the air before I could enjoy my dinner. We were staying at The Stratosphere, the tallest building in town. We were headed for The Top of The World Restaurant 800 feet above ground level.

THE LOTUS GENERATION

The lift doors opened with barely a whisper and a smartly dressed middle aged man smiled invitingly at us as he beckoned us into the cavernous space. Within a heartbeat the doors opened and we were being ushered out into the restaurant by the maître d.

We were seated at a delightful table overlooking the Strip and as I was wriggling comfortably back in my seat and looking around at our fellow diners I heard my husband say politely, " Hello there sir, would you mind moving us from this table as I feel we are far too near the kitchen."

The handsome young waiter who could hardly contain his mirth then replied politely "If you would like to wait there for a few more moments' sir, you will find the kitchen will disappear from view as we are in a revolving restaurant."

My husband thought that was hilarious and was still chuckling when he began to study the capacious menu.

We eventually decided on the four course tasting menu. Grant had rich Lobster bisque and I had my usual Caesar salad. The second course was a no brainer; we both opted for the lump crab cakes with green papaya kimchee.

I was not sure I had ever had kimchee but spicy, fermented pickle tasted fine. The third course was the most delicious grilled centre cut fillet with red wine sauce and wild mushrooms. For desert we had a mini duo each which gave us a taste of all things chocolate, fruit and meringue.

We had the wine recommended with each course as well as the aperitif and liqueurs. When I got up to visit the powder room I was not sure whether it was me or the revolving restaurant that was moving.

Grant went out to see where thrill rides went. There was Sky Jump Las Vegas, Big Shot, at over 1000 feet it is the highest thrill ride in the world, then Insanity and Scream. I decided to have a restorative cup of coffee whilst staring blankly at him through the window, as I was not sure he should have done this. I had gone past him three times before he came back in to join me.

Earlier on in the day as we arrived we had jumped in a taxi at LAX and struck gold with our taxi driver. When he pulled up at our hotel he asked if we would like him to carry our bags in. When we answered in the affirmative he went straight passed the snaking queue waiting at the check in desk. He took us round the corner to the executive desk. My husband asked the young women if we could have a nice room as we were both very tired from all the travelling. She handed the key to him saying "You will be very happy with this one, sir". Anthony, as we had now come to know him, took our cases up to our room.

Whilst Grant thanked him profusely and gave him an appropriate gratuity I had a look around the suite. The whole thing was amazing but the bathroom was divine.

A round whirl pool bath with a 360 degree view of Las Vegas is the epitome of luxury in my experience.

CHAPTER 74
Is That Really You Elvis?

We are all stars and we deserve to twinkle.
Marilyn Monroe

The next morning we got up early, had breakfast in our room and made our way through the already buzzing casino and out into the morning air. We hailed a taxi as we were going to the shopping mall. We knew we were having a brand new grandson in the next few weeks so we shopped for him and the other four children.

We spent a while in a huge jewellers and Grant had a new wedding ring to replace the platinum one he had lost years before. I was a little overcome with the heat that day and so we headed back early to the hotel for a snooze.

I lay on the bed in torpor and really would have liked to stay in bed all evening. Grant was spruced up and ready to go by seven so I suggested he went down to the casino and I would meet him down there.

I pulled myself together and then wandered down to the casino. We went for a delicious supper and then Grant said he had a big surprise for me.

We were going to see an Elvis show.

THE LOTUS GENERATION

My husband and I agree about most things including how to raise a family, where to go on holiday, and what is humorous. We are very well suited except for anything musical. Basically I hate what he likes and he cannot understand my taste at all. Nowhere is the chasm greatest or do we clash more than with Elvis Presley. He loves his music and I find some of the slow numbers make me want to lie on the floor and start sobbing hysterically.

Anyway I am nothing if not a trouper so nine pm saw me sitting in the front row with two hours of Elvis impersonation to look forward to.

We were seated near the aisle of the theatre and the manager came to ask Grant to be sure to keep his arm in, as the star of the night was going to run past us on to the stage. Apparently he was quite a large man and once he had begun his run nothing could stop him and it just might all end in tears.

Actually to be fair he was amazing but I was so grateful when it finally stopped and the thudding in my head began to subside.

CHAPTER 75
A New Handbag At Lax

The most important thing is to enjoy your life, to be happy, that's all that matters.

Audrey Hepburn

We took our leave of that splendid hotel room, waved goodbye to Las Vegas and hopped on the forty five minute plane journey to Los Angeles.

I love LAX airport because if you stand still for a moment all human life passes you by. It was in a moment of reflection that into my field of vision appeared the most gorgeous handbag that I had ever seen.

This was a proper ladies handbag that Audrey Hepburn would have worn, perched on her arm as she went about her day. It was a darling, dainty handbag to hold a lipstick, tiny purse and tissues. Wrong, wrong for me on every level as I needed room for a computer, children's toys, chocolate, reams of paper and pens, a huge bunch of keys, two purses and three pairs of glasses.

Unsuitable for the real me but perfect for my imaginary me who was always perfectly turned out, even-tempered and graceful. With constant *bon mots* falling from her perfectly arranged lips that always had just the right amount of lipstick on.

The only quote of Audrey Hepburn's that came into my mind then was "Happiness is health and a short term memory."

I liked the health bit but was not sure about a short term memory as it would not be any good in my line of work.

My husband found me waiting, whilst the perfect cream bag was being wrapped perfectly in copious amounts of matching tissue.

He grabbed my hand and yelled "This plane is going to go without us."

I smiled my thanks grabbed my card and treasured handbag. As I began to run like the wind, I could saw I swear I saw Audrey smiling from a distance.

We arrived back in UK and after a lovely visit with the family in England, made our way to get the plane back to Alicante airport. We picked up the car and made our way home in the sunshine and I was glad I had another week off work.

We had spent the most wonderful couple of weeks and I wanted to be able to remember it all at my leisure.

CHAPTER 76
Some Great Years And A Long Lie Down

A smart girl leaves before she is left.
Marilyn Monroe

There is a special sunshine sensation that overtakes your whole being when you are momentarily freed from the drudgery of employment and domesticity.

It is that "the sun is always shining here and I can rule the world" notion that should be ignored at all costs. Ignored that is until you have been back home living your life for three months and made a sensible plan.

THE LOTUS GENERATION

We had been living in Spain for a few years and I loved the whole thing, the weather, the people and my work which took me all over the world. We had sold our family home in Surrey and intended to buy a villa in Spain and home nearer London when we had time to go house hunting.

Things were all going swimmingly in my life. I was running training courses with my colleague and dear friend Francesca in beautiful rural locations. I was working in a picturesque clinic by the ocean and had a multinational client base. I had also set up an online retail company dealing in fair trade and ethical products. I was also out every night with my husband, sister and her husband eating, drinking, dancing and generally having a merry old time.

I was definitely the ruler of my world and I woke up every day in the sunshine ready to begin another perfect day.

However I had forgotten a cardinal rule. When this invincible sensation overtakes you, go home and make a sensible plan. I had also forgotten that I had been diagnosed with Multiple Sclerosis in my twenties and the harder I worked then I was more likely to suffer a relapse.

I had been working in London with Francesca and then rushed back to Spain to run a training course. The course was for twelve people and it was going well but then I began to feel very strange. I was tired, dizzy and it took every fibre of my being to get through until the end of the week.

When I got home I went straight to bed and there I remained for many months. I had had a full-blown relapse and I was not going anywhere in a hurry.

Grant had not worked since we had been in Spain and continued with his social routine but I was no fun at all as a companion. I could not walk very far, so the beach or even a drive in the car was out of the question.

That summer was very hot but I just hoped that my health would improve and life would start to get better for us both. I lay every day on the sofa in the sitting room as it was the only place we had air conditioning.

One day my sister knocked on the door and I could tell by the look on her face that she had something to tell me. "I am going back to live in England" she explained "I have been here much longer than you and it's time for me to go home"

I was lying on the sofa at the time and tried hard to struggle to my feet. "Where are you going to go?" I said visibly trying to lower my eyebrows from the elevated place that they had risen to. "I am going to look after my grandson George, as my daughter Claire is going back to work." she said and next day she was gone.

I had not realised how much I relied on her and I missed her terribly. I still could not get about much and had cancelled most of my work commitments.

I began to wonder if I would ever be well enough to work again and worried for the first time about the future.

CHAPTER 77
Would You Like To Come Back?

Because of this, originality consists in returning to the origin.
Antonio Gaudi

A couple of weeks later our oldest son Theo came out to Spain and said "I would like you to come back to England to live. I have just bought a lovely little house for you near the cathedral. I want you to move in there because we are all worried about your health."

We thanked him for his wonderfully generous offer and told him we would think about this overnight and let him know the next day. Grant took him to Valencia airport for his flight home.

When he got home Grant rubbed his hands together and said "Well should we start packing?" I did not have enough energy to get from the kitchen to the veranda and told him I needed a little time to think about it.

I loved my life in Spain but it was based upon being able to work long hours and enjoy life, not being incapacitated and miserable. The financial crisis was worldwide and although we read about its effects in other places it was a reality for the people in Spain. The cost of living in Spain had rocketed, the Euro had risen against Stirling and people's mind-set had changed regarding the issue of spending money on themselves.

I lay awake that night and eventually decided that we would be better off in England. Better off on the balance of probabilities, whatever they were?

We packed up some of our things to take back to England. We put some things in storage and gave lots of things to a Spanish children's charity that I had been involved with.

We slammed the storage door on our possessions that we were leaving behind including Grant's red Alfa Romeo that we had had such fun in driving along the coastal roads.

Saying goodbye to our friends and colleagues was difficult but the journey home was fine in the end. We stopped at the city of Girona, in the Catalan region of Spain for the first night.

I had booked accommodation in the castle but we could not find the right road to take us high above the city. Grant stopped a policeman and in his faltering Spanish asked for directions. The policeman smiled and drove us through the city gates and to a picturesque destination we would never had found without his kindness.

Two minutes' walk from our spacious hotel suite we found a restaurant and wandered in. We opted for the seven course tasting menu and had the most wonderful meal that we had eaten in all the time we were in Spain. Prawns, squid, rabbit and truffle dishes were some of that most memorable experience

The next night we stopped somewhere in France as we were very tired. The sign said "The Birthplace of the Lady that invented the Tarte Tatin." How quaint, we thought as we were shown up to our room. The hotel was old with little rabbit warren corridors and so we were struck completely speechless when Madame opened the door to the room.

It was James Bond's lair from the 1970s. Red, fluffy shag carpet covered the floor and the walls. I went into the bathroom to look and the red carpet covered the sides of the large round bath as well. We were stuck in a seventies time warp. A huge round water bed and glass and chrome as far as the eye could see. The space was enormous, across the whole of the house. Plants hung from the ceilings in macramé holders and space ship shaped lights were everywhere.

After we had stopped laughing we went downstairs to see what the restaurant was like. Perfect, was the answer as the seven course menu ending with the famous Tarte Tatin was sublime?

We did not sleep very well as the water bed sensation made us both a little bilious and red is not the most restful of colours.

We paid the very reasonable bill the next morning and as we drove through the local villages Grant remarked "The Tarte Tatin lady must have moved house a lot."

"Why?" I asked with my eyes firmly closed.

"That is the twelfth place I have seen that says she actually lived in that house"

We were in good spirits as we boarded the euro star shuttle and were looking forward most of all to seeing the family.

As we drove into the Suffolk town that was to be our new home it started to snow heavily and I wondered if it was a metaphor for the next phase of our life.

CHAPTER 78
Remind Me Where We Are

In the language of flowers a bunch of daffodils means Joy and Happiness.
Anon.

Our lovely little house was within the sound of the charming bells of the magnificent cathedral, six churches and the tinkling chimes of the clock over Moyses Hall Museum.

It was lovely being near my oldest son's children. The little ones were only two months and twenty months when we moved back and I loved having them over to our little house. Their older daughter Jessica loved sleepovers and I spent many hours reading and baking with her. I could not walk very far as I was still in the grip of the MS relapse but I tried to make visits fun.

We both missed the sunshine in the grip of that freezing first winter but being back near the family more than made up for it. The

THE LOTUS GENERATION

human condition means that very quickly the unfamiliar becomes familiar and a sense of normality prevails.

Twice a week there was a large market dating back centuries. The flower selling with their magnificent displays meant that I could fill my houses with whatever was in season for less than £10 a week.

Spring meant cream vases, full of sweet smelling lilac or blue hyacinths for the sitting room. The door to this room at the front of the house was mostly kept closed and the perfume of the hyacinths mixed with the faint scent of lavender polish from the antique desk brought back memories of my grandmother's elegant old house.

Daffodils and jonquils of every shade of yellow and white filled every surface in the kitchen. The family joke was that you could never find a jug for the custard, gravy or mint sauce, as they were all full of daffodils.

My favourite flower receptacle was a blue and white striped jug, chipped and a little bashed round the edges over the years. It had belonged to my Great Grandmother Hannah and it always took pride of place on my kitchen table wherever I lived.

Hannah had taught me the art of flower arranging when I was small. She had owned a magnificent hotel and left most jobs to the staff, but the flowers were her domain even into her eighties.

Each spring the rows of tulips were breathtaking and I would stand and chat to the lovely, lady flower seller whilst making my choice. She would always laugh when I asked for the same thing. "Arms full of orange parrot tulips to go. Please"

For summer, with its warmer weather, I brought out my mother's crystal vases and bought fat pink peonies, majestic white lilies, and lilac phlox for the dining room. White pottery jugs held huge orange marigolds on the kitchen window ledge and pine dresser.

I love the smell of autumn bonfires and wet leaves. My favourite flowers for the house were my antique Chinese blue vases either side of the mantelpiece, filled with bright yellow, white and bronze chrysanthemums. I also loved to place huge purple pots of them by the front door for passers-by to enjoy.

The things I loved most in autumn were the fat orange pumpkins I could use as doorstops whilst they waited to be transformed by little hands into lanterns for a Halloween treat.

Winter for me has always meant poinsettias. Large red ones, of course either side of the dining room fireplace but also pink and cream ones scattered about the house. On the console table stood an African violet, watered carefully, to avoid splashing the leaves and a Christmas cactus with its fat pink buds.

Then just before Christmas, miraculously the perfect daffodils arrive again. In a perfect slender vase, looking for all the world like forced rhubarb stands a tiny bunch of hope for the coming year.

CHAPTER 79
The Mystery Of The Exploding Yoghurt Pot

"Anyone for tennis?"
Anon.

I was determined to get fit and I tried to swim every week and do at least one class of Pilates with my friends. Our aqua aerobics lessons usually ended in uproar as the teacher was very strict and we were all ladies of a certain age not used to be told what to do.

The lessons usually ended with a cheerful pub lunch where we undid all the good work swimming had just done. I tried to walk into town at least three times a week to do some shopping and this was where my latest adventure began.

I come from a very political family and so I had met most of the Labour Party front bench at one time or another. My father had been a trade union Leader and ran the Labour Party in the Northern town in which we lived.

My father is a very amenable man and takes people as he finds them, still active in his nineties. My mother was another matter and held a real grudge against Margaret Thatcher and her acolytes all her life for what they had done to the miners.

One day I was coming out of Marks and Spencer's food hall when a very charming elderly chap in a flat cap held open the door for me. I thanked him and we chatted for a while about the weather. People may change but their voices rarely do and as I walked away I thought to myself, "I am sure I know him".

THE LOTUS GENERATION

As I was putting my shopping away it came to me "I know who that was, it was Norman Tebbit." He was a member of Mrs Thatcher's government of the 1970s and 1980s. He was actually the man who had told people to get on their bikes to look for work, which had incensed my mother!

As I filled the fridge with fruit and vegetables I thought about my mother. I actually said "Gosh mum if you could have seen me today" as I squashed the last pot of Greek yoghurt into the fridge.

I woke up to the sound of our little Bichon dog Stella barking. I pulled my new dressing gown over my nightie and put my feet in my slippers. I crept down the stairs. She seemed fine in her basket so I turned to go back up to bed. Then I noticed a new four pint carton of milk that had been left out of the fridge. I leant across the cabinet to get it and walked back to the fridge.

As I opened the fridge door the large, renegade carton of yoghurt that been waiting, carefully balanced, flew out of the fridge and hit me squarely in the chest. Before I could grab it, it bounced off my bath robe and on to the floor relieving itself of its lid and discharged its contents far and wide. No part of the kitchen escaped the pine dresser with my Delph blue pottery; the terracotta floor tiles, the ceiling and the whole of me including my recently washed hair were saturated.

I breathed deeply and reached across for some kitchen roll and bent down to wipe the floor. In to this mess bounced a little white gleeful dog.

"Could this get any worse?" I said to myself through gritted teeth. Well actually yes it could.

The fridge door was open when I bent down but gravity started to slowly close it. It jammed itself firmly into my back as I was bent double. I could not move either backwards or forwards. I wriggled and jiggled and my little dog kept bringing a green tennis ball to throw.

Finally, I forced my way back up vertically and then waited a moment for the dizziness to pass. Using all the kitchen towels to clean the floor and the sides of the dresser I said to myself "I will do it properly in the morning but first I must put all this in the washing machine now"

THE LOTUS GENERATION

I walked through to the laundry room and opened the door of the machine. I shoved the towels in but it did not make a full wash. Finally I looked down and noticed how much of the horrible white yoghurt gunge was all over me. Then I stood pensively making a decision.

"Oh blow it" I said to myself, "nothing ventured, nothing gained."

I carefully took off all my yoghurt drenched night clothes and stuffed them into the washing machine.

Satisfied that I had a full wash, I turned the light off and padded quickly through the kitchen. As I passed the fridge my bare feet slid on the slippery floor and sent me flying onto my back.

I lay there with the wind knocked out of me not knowing whether to laugh or cry.

Stella, the bichon fris was so excited that I was down at her level and ran to get the green tennis ball and placed it carefully on my expansive chest. Grant hearing a loud bang in the middle of the night grabbed the nearest defensive implement he could find which just happened to be an old tennis racket.

As he put his head tentatively round the kitchen door he found his yoghurt strewn, naked wife lying on the floor holding a tennis ball. He swung his racket in the air and said "Fancy a game, love?"

The next day as we cleaned the kitchen Grant said "I wonder if your mother did this because you were seen cavorting with the enemy".

I would normally have laughed at this suggestion but I felt that the extra pressure that this would put on my bruised coccyx would not be sensible.

I really felt that my bottom was beginning to bruise badly. When I asked him to look, Grant did make me laugh because he gave me an old fashioned look and asked "Is it compulsory? "When I finally stopped complaining and went along for an x ray, it turned out I had chipped my coccyx.

All I can say about that little incident is Ouch!

CHAPTER 80
Ethical, Fairtrade And Eco Friendly

For fast acting relief try slowing down.
Lily Tomlin

I opened an office and warehouse in the town for my burgeoning on-line store. We sold everything that was eco-friendly, organic, fair trade or ethical. We had started with a few bars of handmade soap and some children's clothes made locally in Spain. Our rapidly growing beauty section was my favourite as I got to go to the factories to see how things were made and test all the products. I also loved our elegant home ware department. I had had such a good time travelling in Europe to find the most exquisite things to sell.

I had always had an interest in fair-trade products. My mother Mona had been born before her time. She was slender as a bean pole when to be fully figured was the fashion and her ideas on recycling and fair wages, for everyone including those in poor countries, were seen as frankly crazy in the 1940s and 1950s.

Our home was different to other peoples as we always had to think of others before ourselves. Nothing was ever wasted and every penny accounted for. When other bins were overflowing ours contained a few washed and squashed tins. Flowers, fruit and vegetable peelings went on the compost and paper, string, and scraps of material were all saved in a drawer for another day.

Any grocery shopping trip was always carefully planned. One had to leave at the crack of dawn so as to procure the freshest goods. Products from South Africa were definitely banned because of apartheid and any change had to be accounted for to the exact penny.

My dear mother cared about the environment so much and turned lights and radiators off the minute she left the room. Running water was not allowed when you brushed your teeth and food was never to be left on your plate.

I agreed with a lot of her ideas on the environment and fair trade but when I married I always ran a home that was frankly just the opposite of the one I grew up in. Everything in my house was plentiful, from food and time to laughter and joy.

THE LOTUS GENERATION

I think maybe it was just the difference between raising your children in the 1950s to being a mother in the1970s.

I awoke every day full of excitement about what the new day's business would bring. Early mornings were spent at home checking the orders that had come in overnight, then to the office for meetings with staff. The afternoons were for visits to suppliers and helping send parcels out to customers from all over the world.

I loved being my own boss as it allowed me to take time off to go to the gym,swimming or pick the children up from school. Also when I felt unwell I could always work from home.

I decided to keep part of my business in Spain and usually spoke to someone out there most days. Ella and Georgina ran my websites and internet business and whatever I asked of them, they came up with straight away with a smile.

During the time we lived in Suffolk I was still able to do my coaching and run some training courses. I enjoyed travelling to Ireland to help run NLP courses there with Lydia who I met in London. The countryside around Cork is splendid and the hospitality shown to us by Lydia and Liam was heart-warming.

In an evening I loved the Sky Arts channel that had appeared in my life in 2007. I enjoyed the idea of being able to view so many eclectic performances across all genres. On the other hand I could be found watching the inimitable Judge Judy Sheindlin or the magnificent Oprah Winfrey on a loop whilst I was working. I absolutely loved their advice and views on life in general.

I loved all my different projects but the spectre of exhaustion from MS was always just about to raise its unwelcome head and had to be fought with every endeavour.

CHAPTER 81
Where Have All The Birds Gone?

Each bird must sing with his own throat.
Henrik Ibsen

Living in the town has its advantages such as proximity to the theatre, cinema and music venues. Evening post prandial walks could end with a pint and a glass of wine at a local hostelry if you were so inclined. Popping to Waitrose or Marks and Spencer's for something you have forgotten took ten minutes.

The one down side for me meant that we only had a tiny courtyard. When we moved in I thought that I would miss the space as we had always had large gardens and it had always been my thinking chamber and outdoor gym rolled into one.

I worked hard on the courtyard and it became beautiful with an ever changing colour display. I planted a wisteria and it flew up the side of the house and its reams of mauve flowers were magnificent in the southerly sun.

I planted fig trees in the sun and apples and pears in the shade by the shed. Our house had been a tiny vicarage and the upside down house next door had been a church. The elegant and cheerful nonagenarian lady who lived next door loved flowers. Her French windows were twenty feet above my courtyard and we waved hello and discussed the weather every morning.

I sent clouds of pale pink rambling roses and lilac early flowering clematis up through the old holly tree. The view from on high was spectacular and it pleased her immensely. Everything was in pots including large chunks of bamboo that rustled in the breeze and gave the arbour some structure.

I insisted on bringing my pink marble dining table back from Spain and the only place we had room for it was outside. The rain and the sun had disturbed its patina but that only added to its charm. When you closed your eyes on a sunny day, whilst drinking a glass of cooling lemonade, you could be transported to anywhere in the world.

I always had the back door open because I love the sound of church bells. The mystical thought that for centuries they were the only call to prayer for the congregation was enlivening.

The one thing I really missed though was the sound of the birds. I had always derived great pleasure from the garden birds and enrolled all the little ones in the RSPB when they were old enough to understand. However, I discovered that living in the centre of a town meant that most houses had cats and the feline creatures near us ruled the roost as they prowled around with their heads held high. I think that counted for the bird's demise but also we were in the middle of a huge arable area where growing the crops was everything and chemical fertilisers were regularly sprayed without compunction.

The music was a different story however. We loved to visit the churches and particularly the cathedral for exquisite classical concerts. A new music venue opened and lots of groups from our youth suddenly appeared for our delectation. The summer festival was a tapestry of sounds, heard not only by the people who had paid to go in the Abbey Gardens but by the whole town as well.

It was such fun to take the children with us to concerts. Ten year old Felix's face when he realised that he would have to sit through an hour of opera was a picture.

He did however enjoy the Gilbert and Sullivan portion and went out humming "A policeman's lot is not a happy one."

CHAPTER 82
I Will Just Stay Down Here, Thank You

Living involves tearing up one rough draft after another.
Anon.

The misty, murky whiteout was slowly enveloping me in its tendrils and hazy amorphous shapes were sliding across the edges of my vision. I had the uncomfortable feeling that I was lying by the side of a lake on a cool, foggy day

I knew something was very wrong but in the far off place I was in it did not seem to matter. Then a bell began to ring, quietly at first and then it stopped without warning. The insistent noise had wakened me from my reverie and I tried to look around. My eyes began to focus and I realised my head was at an awkward angle.

THE LOTUS GENERATION

I realised then that I was on my bedroom floor trapped between the bed and the heavy mahogany dresser. The bell started again louder this time and then I moved my head. The ringing was the phone, which had fallen to the floor with me.

"Hello" I croaked "Oh, thank goodness" said Miranda my daughter. "Whatever is happening?"

"I don't know" I managed to murmur. My mouth was so dry. "Stay on the line" she commanded "and promise, promise me, Mum, that you will stay awake."

It might have been five minutes later or it might have been five hours I have no way of knowing. I came to and found my husband was standing over me peering, closely followed by the paramedics. With a lot of kerfuffle I was soon back in the hospital I had left a few hours earlier.

I had been feeling ill for months and had gone backwards and forwards between specialists. I had been in the emergency room of the hospital for five hours the day before because I had been haemorrhaging for some time. I was waiting for a bed in the ward when a new doctor had come to tell me that I could go home.

The nurse who had been with me all afternoon tried to argue but he said the decision had been made. I did not sleep much in the night because of terrible pain but I just assumed it would diminish. Doctors know what they are doing, don't they?

The next morning Grant my husband had a meeting in town and had asked me if I was feeling better. "I am fine, just go" was the answer I gave in the manner of women everywhere, although I must admit I was hoping he would stay with me.

I drifted back off but when I had tried to get out of bed, because I was so weak through lack of blood, I had just collapsed on to the floor.

My daughter who lived a hundred miles away had rung the hospital and then spoken sharply to her father. He was on a train but got off at the next stop, turned round and arrived at the same time as the ambulance.

Once I was back at the hospital they began a barrage of tests. I had been lying upside down on one machine for some considerable time and I asked if I could go to the bathroom. A nurse came by and

THE LOTUS GENERATION

pushed me in a wheelchair to a facility. After pushing the chair right up to the sink she walked away saying rather insouciantly "I'll be back"

Grant, my husband of many years stood pale and wan by my side." I will give you some privacy" he whispered and shut the door behind him.

"Privacy, privacy" I would have fumed if I had felt well enough "I don't need privacy, I need you to help me, if you would not mind".

I was calm, peaceful and relaxed under a straw parasol on my favourite Spanish beach. I was wearing my beautiful lilac swimsuit and matching sarong. The weather was perfect, sunny but with a breeze that caressed my cheek. I was hoping the waiter would soon bring out my order of a gin and tonic and bowl of olives.

"Mm..... Perfect life does not get any better than this" I thought as I wriggled down on my sunbed. "Well it would be perfect if the breeze stopped caressing my cheek so insistently.

I heard my name being called from the far side of the beach and I reluctantly forced my eyes open. Six pairs of eyes I did not recognise were staying back at me. The owner of the blue eyes, who appeared to be the bossiest by far, was asking me if I was alright. Why would I not be alright on this lovely...actually it was not a beach, it was a dusty, grey, tiled lavatory floor.

I closed my eyes to go back to Spain but they were not having any of it.

I had fainted because I had lost so much blood, knocked myself out and fallen so hard behind the door that they actually had to take it off to get to me.

My husband said "I heard a bang and so I called for help". It was a good job I was so weak otherwise I might have been forced to give him an overdue piece of my mind.

By the end of that day I knew that I had concussion and a large bump on my head. I was also in dire need of a hysterectomy but I had developed such severe pancreatitis in the afternoon that any surgery would have to wait a while until I was stabilised.

I lay in a room on my own with the blinds down and I cannot really tell you how I felt as I was on so much medication that one day morphed into another and then another.

CHAPTER 83
Forty-Two Goes Pop!

Grandmothers are just antique little girls.
Anon.

Three weeks later after having surgery I was allowed home with instructions to take great care of myself. I still needed other work done including the removal of my recalcitrant gall bladder.

Matron came to see me and said "You have forty plus stitches but they are soluble so don't worry about them."

About two weeks later the scar was really smarting so I asked Grant if he would have a look. I pulled my nightgown up with as much modesty as I could muster because I was still at bit miffed with him.

He stood with his hand on his hips staring at the offending scar. Finally he said "Soluble mm, unless the laws of physics have changed these stiches are going to be around at the next millennium."

There were actually forty two metal clamps holding my scar together and they needed to be taken out pronto. A quick visit to the hospital ended with a lot of "oohing and aahing" from me as the pliers had to be jiggled first this way and that.

Finally I was on my way back home with tears still smarting in my eyes.

About a week later I was looking after my four year old granddaughter Ruby and three year old grandson Oscar. The weather was glorious so when Grant came home we decided to go for a walk. I was a little tired on the way home so we stopped at the coffee shop.

Grant said to me "You stay out here with children and I will go inside and get the coffees and ice cream." The children and I settled ourselves on the ubiquitous white plastic chairs that were on the piazza. I got colouring books and crayons out of my Mary Poppins bag and they leaned peacefully on the table drawing away to their hearts content.

All was well until Oscar needed the blue crayon. I was sitting peacefully one minute looking over the top of my sunglasses at my lovely family and the next minute I was flying through the air like a cartoon character. Oscar had stood up to reach for the crayon and in a millisecond was starting to overbalance.

With a basic primeval instinct, I was going to stop him from hitting the floor. Of course I caught him and it was smiles all around as Granddad came out with the ice cream.

This is the kind of domestic incident that happens every day all over the world with small children.

After we drove them home I said quietly to Grant "Would you mind driving home via the hospital?"

As I had flown through the air like Super granny I felt my recently unstitched scar go pop, pop, and pop.! Forty two times...They took one look and readmitted me. The good news was that as they sewed me up again they were able to complete all the other surgery including removing my gall bladder.

Since then I have found I have really had no use for it except when anybody is offering me fish and chips.

I always put my hand up in the manner of a traffic policeman say "Not for me thank you!"

Not long after this we were walking in the gardens near the Cathedral. It was the first day of the annual Christmas Fayre and at seven am there were people everywhere.

We had four small grandchildren who had stayed the night and two dogs with us. The path down to the river and the swing park was overlaid with leads and wires for the attractions and were covered with rubber covers. A petite whey faced lady was pushing a large moustached gentleman complete with trilby, along in a wheelchair.

As they got level with us the lady managed to get the wheelchair stuck on the lead cover. Quick as a flash my husband Grant came to her aid. She stood aside as my husband wiggled the wheelchair and its incumbent and with a cheery "Voila" set it free in one bound.

The distracted wife smiled a wan smile of appreciation; from where I was I could not see the expression on the man's face.

She walked away quickly and as we had small children and dogs with us our pace was sedentary. "Hey, look at that" said Grant pointing into distance.

Every time the petite lady reached another obstacle her large, sedentary husband stepped smartly out of the wheelchair, walked a few paces and then got back in again when she had negotiated the hurdle....

CHAPTER 84
The Christmas Fayre

Christmas is not so much about opening presents as about opening hearts.
Anon.

The Christmas Fayre was a delight for the senses and attracted many thousands of visitors and stall holders from around Great Britain, Europe and beyond. As darkness fell the strings of sparkling lights looked spectacular in shades of red and white, green and blue. Along the cobbled street in front of the Cathedral and the Norman tower, famous and novice bands were setting up their stages to rouse the night away.

The Buttermarket was full of wonderful smelling stalls selling all kinds of provisions from homemade pies and cakes to hot cider and Gluwein .The most popular inhabitant of the gardens was of course Father Christmas. However everyone in the snaking queue agreed that the old potting shed where he resided was not very festive.

The Athenaeum with its spectacular Georgian chandeliers housed the artists, glass makers and myriad beautifully designed treasures all to be bought for a realistic price. We had started to collect a local artist and this year we bought a winter scene with partridges flying across the skyline.

Next morning we got up early to take the children on the merry go rounds as it had been deemed too busy by their father the night before. We ended a lovely weekend with a trip to the local patisserie where they drank hot chocolate and ate squishy brownies to their hearts content.

After a delightful Christmas had passed, we decided we were going to get fitter. Like lots of other people we had joined a few gyms over the years but then stopped going after six weeks and carried on paying for goodness knows how long.

THE LOTUS GENERATION

There's a swish hotel, in a nearby local village that caters to a large golfing population. They had a fabulous gym and swimming pool and we had looked around before signing up. I completed my induction hour with a wonderful blonde, blue eyed chap called Sven and as I sat red faced and hot we began to chat. To my consternation he began to measure and weigh me whilst asking me about my diet.

To change the subject I asked him what part of Scandinavia his family came from as he had already mentioned his older brother Bjorn. "Croydon" he said and stopped whilst holding dangerous looking fat callipers aloft. "Oh," I said weekly. He smiled and said "My mother is Marjorie and my father is Dennis, but they did like Abba!"

I loved going to the gym whilst my husband walked mile after mile on the treadmill I paced myself leisurely and watched episodes of *This Morning* or *Neighbours* depending on the time of day.

I enjoyed swimming afterwards as long as I did not have to get my hair wet. I know I looked like a little duck with my legs paddling like mad and my head in the air but frankly I did not care.

One sunny Sunday morning I got up early to do some work. I was in my office when I decided to put on some coffee. I walked through to the kitchen and thought about putting a washing machine load in as it was a sunny day for drying.

As I walked back through from the laundry room I spied some plants that needed watering. Still dressed in my nightie I stared out of the French windows and thought "Oh what a perfect day."

The sun was shining on my ancient pine kitchen dresser with its blue and white china melange of interesting new Wedgwood pieces, old flea market Cornish ware finds and ancient and sometimes chipped antiques passed down through my mother's family.

My Grandmother Hester was absolutely wonderful, warm and loving but had a hilarious, explosive temper and some of the things I had inherited from her were subsequently discovered to be stuck together glue. She was an excellent cricketer and her bowling arm was the envy of many. She collected rare porcelain Dresden dolls and blue Spanish Lladro figurines and even the odd one of these was discovered to have a hairline crack on inspection.

THE LOTUS GENERATION

The star of the kitchen show however was a Tiffany lamp that I had owned for years. Various shades of purple, lilac and green glass sent reflective coloured light whirling around the room. The shade was twenty four inches wide and it stood thirty inches high, it was my prize possession carefully carried by my hand in every house move.

I barely noticed that the water needed changing in the round Vera Wang Blanc enamel vase of purple and white parrot tulips standing next to the lamp.

Then I slowly bent down to pick up a lovely Fiscus Benjamina plant that stood proudly on my kitchen floor in its matching pot.

It was heavier than I expected and I reached up to grab the handle of the French windows for support. Somebody who shall remain nameless had left both the doors unlocked last night and as I put my not inconsiderable weight on the handle, both of the doors flew open at once.

I left the kitchen in a hurry that morning in the manner of superman with my nightie billowing out beside me. In fact I felt that I really knew what it was like to fly.

I landed head first in the lavender banging my head on the shed. My knees were grazed on the low brick wall and it took me a while for my head to stop spinning. I decided to be brave in case the people next door had heard the commotion and were looking out of their high French windows.

It wasn't the first time I remembered that I really should start wearing pyjamas to cover my dignity. I finally managed to struggle to my feet and started to brush the mud off my knees. Then a little moan really did escape my lips. It was my thumb on my right hand. Not the beautifully manicured pink gel nail that I always had on, that was intact. It was my actual thumb that was the problem going first this way and that.

You know when you break something the pain does not kick in straight away, it takes a few minutes. It kicked in that day in the time it took me to pour some coffee and take it to my still sleeping husband.

Once he was sitting up I said through my tears "Could you please look at this? He stared for a while recollecting his early golf game. "I think it might be better if you leave it a while to see how it goes" he said lamely.

"Fine" I said I will take myself. So I did, arriving before the nurses at the emergency room. A young doctor said "It needs an X ray" and off I went.

An hour later I met up with him in a small ante room. He was holding the x ray up to the light. "This joint is very much worn" he said to nobody in particular.

"If you look this way my young man" I said with as much dignity as I could muster through a marbled haze of pain "You will notice that the worn thumb joint matches the rest of me "

He burst out laughing and really looked up at me "This thumb is broken in two places but how on earth did you keep that beautifully manicured nail intact."

Two hours later I arrived home with a plaster on my battered digit and heavy duty painkillers. I looked a little ridiculous as for weeks it appeared that I was giving cheery thumbs up signs to all and sundry. Grant having cancelled his golf was very solicitous and offered to cook lunch. I was excused the gym for a month and spent a lot of time watching the shopping channel.

CHAPTER 85
Why Are You In My Bedroom?

To live is so startling; it leaves little time for anything else.
Anon

I was really looking forward to this summer as two of my favourite men in the whole world had planned their weddings just seven days apart.

The first wedding was my brother Harry to his fiancé Anne-Marie in the English Lakes at the end of May. The second was my nephew Rufus' wedding to his fiancée Fiona in Greece the first week in June.

At the beginning of March my daughter Miranda asked me to help her to redecorate the children's bedrooms. I went to stay with her and the family for two wonderful weeks. We had a lot of fun browsing and then choosing curtains and bed linen and it was wonderful to spend some time together.

I went with my oldest grandson Felix to the garden centre to buy some more fish for the garden pond. We carried our carefully chosen precious catch home and then tipped it into the fizzing, dark depths of water beneath the tinkling waterfall.

We hoped the heron that frequented these parts would be kept away by the large plastic heron we had just purchased to confuse her. We knew she could not manage to lift the weighty koi carp but we wanted to give the other fish time to grow.

Grant and I had happily sploshed our ancient goldfish in the pond when they moved into this lovely house. Goldie and Silver had lived for years in our farmhouse kitchen but had grown exponentially in the last few years.

One day, years before I was standing at the back door of my daughter's house holding blonde haired, two year old Felix, in my arms. My daughter Miranda had been feeding the koi carp and had just joined us in the kitchen doorway.

Suddenly it went dark and a large heron swooped down. Of all the fish in the pond to take that day, when he lifted his large beak it contained the only shimmering, silver goldfish in the land. Silver, the goldfish had turned that amazing colour the day after we won him at the country fair.

Felix screeched "Oh Mummy, where is Silver going?" and burst into tears.

My quick thinking daughter replied with insouciance "Actually darling today is a wedding day for silver goldfish and the heron has been chosen to escort him to meet his bride"

Felix tears turned into smiles and he ran to play on the swing. "Where did that idea come from?" I asked his Mum.

"Absolutely no idea, I just heard my mouth say the words" she laughed and went to make some tea.

As we were having afternoon tea with Felix and Ellie and their friends I thought how beautiful this garden was, surrounded by ancient rhododendrons in full bloom in verdant English woodland.

I left the next day and when I returned home I began to feel strangely chilly and lethargic. I had also developed a really sore

THE LOTUS GENERATION

throat. Apparently I had caught tonsillitis from somewhere. It could have been the train, the garden centre, the school, outer space, where does one catch these things?

So began the oddest six weeks of my life. One night I woke up to find Gillian, my wonderful GP in the bedroom staring at me. Grant had called her out because as he said "You were talking even faster than usual" She explained to me that she was admitting me to hospital in the middle of the night because my temperature was so high and I was absolutely incoherent.

I was admitted to a general ward and as I drifted in and out of consciousness they continually pumped me full of stronger and stronger antibiotics. Eventually because nothing was working they filled me full of steroids. After about a week the doctors decided I needed exercise so they let me walk about attached to a drip.

The general ward I was in included women from sixteen to ninety six. During the day a sweet old lady called Rose was admitted to the corner bed in the ward. At least I thought she was sweet until her daughter-in-law came to visit and Rose was very mean to her. "Ouch" I thought and went on talking to my visitors.

The doctors were having trouble stabilising my infection so I decided, as I could not do anything about it, that I would just relax. It was three am and I was fast asleep when a young woman was admitted and she was very upset, sobbing uncontrollably. A very tall and very kind nurse called Gavin was dealing with her. I felt very thirsty and so I raised myself on one elbow to get a drink of water; it was difficult as I was still attached to a drip in both arms.

I glanced around in the gloom and out of the corner of my eye I saw Rose, the old lady in the corner launch herself like an Excocet missile at Nurse Gavin's back. With a whoop and a holler she pushed him aside and screaming loudly started to attack the sobbing young women for "making too much noise."

I leapt out of bed to try to help but could not as I was tied to machines. "Think, think, and think" I said to myself "You know how to deal with this."

I heard my voice boom through the air loudly "Excuse me; Rose is there a recipe for chocolate cake in your *Women's Weekly*?"

THE LOTUS GENERATION

as I had noticed that her daughter in law had brought her a copy that day.

The question stopped her mind in its tracks and she gave up fighting and turned to face me across the ward.

"Yes, there is I will get it for you" she said politely, turning. Then her face changed to a furious mask.

"I know it's you" she yelled. "That machine you are attached to is a bomb. I can hear it ticking."

I looked across to my right and I could see a row of nurses and orderlies staring at the tableaux from behind the door. I turned to Gavin and said "Please try and get the young woman out of here" and he started to push her bed towards the doorway.

I then realised two things at the same time. One was that I was no longer attached to one of my machines and the other was that Rose was beginning to get undressed.

Nurse Gavin got the young woman's metal bed through the door and I then picked up a blanket and started to walk towards Rose. She was convinced I was a bomb but I persuaded her that the blanket was bombproof and managed to get it so that it covered her modesty.

She talked for a while about war and she finally calmed down and got back in bed and soon a small snore whistled through her pursed lips.

Soon people started filing back in the ward and all returned to normal.

I lay there with my heart pounding and then it only seemed two minutes later before I was being woken by a lady with the breakfast trolley.

CHAPTER 86
Thank You For Helping My Daughter

Life is simple. It's just not easy.
Anon.

The young woman's mother came to thank me the next day for helping her daughter. By late afternoon it was obvious I had a real problem with my arm where the drip had been dragged out. I had developed severe cellulitis in my arm and it was getting worse and I was confined to bed with even bigger doses of stronger antibiotics.

I started to drift in and out of consciousness and was sent for a lumbar puncture and then I think I was in a room on my own. In my conscious moments I did begin to wonder how anyone could get so sick from a sore throat. I knew the answer of course having MS can give you a compromised immune system. I was covered in bruises and holes from all the blood tests and drips that had been attached to me

A few days later I awoke to realise I was in a different place. I looked around and realised that I could only see very old ladies, then realised I was in a geriatric ward as there was no room anywhere else. I could not sit up and a very busy but bossy nurse came along and fed me a spoonful of red hot porridge that was sitting on the side. When I choked and coughed she just glared at me and slammed it down on the locker.

A young nurse in his twenties came along and cooled it for me and then fed me with a teaspoon and talked to me gently. He came back ten minutes later with a cool coffee and a bendy straw and stayed patiently until I had finished. When he came round later in the day I thanked him and told him what a difference he had made to my welfare that miserable morning.

I could see the funny side of my situation later that day when the doctors and nurses came to do the ward rounds. The assembled group of medics swished a thin, faded cotton curtain across the end of the bed and began an esoteric discussion about me as though I was completely deaf and daft.

"I can hear exactly what you are saying you know" I said cheerily. Two seconds later a young doctor peered through a chink in the curtains and winked at me.

I lay in bed for two days before I was allowed to get up. I never closed my eyes during this time as the old ladies just talked saying the same things over and over and mostly memories of childhood.

The eighty five year old retired geography mistress in the next bed recited the same lesson about precipitation over and over again. Long forgotten detailed discussions with their mothers or teachers filled the long small hours and my heart went out to them.

When I was finally allowed to walk about, pushing a drip on a stand, I realised that the doors to the ward were firmly locked. Whether that was to keep people in or out I never discovered.

I was finally allowed out four days before my brother's wedding. I was left with many questions. How do you get so ill with tonsillitis that you need six weeks in hospital? How do the hospital staff do such an amazing job week in and week out? Why do we treat our old and vulnerable people differently to everyone else? I felt as though I had gazed through a time warped looking glass to see how it was be to be an old lady...

As soon as I had got home I jumped on the scales expecting to have lost at least a stone. A combination of calories fed intravenously and not moving a muscle for six weeks meant I had not lost even a pound.

I spent the next three days trying to get organised for the two weddings that I was determined to attend. I still felt very dizzy and disorientated but Grant cheekily remarked most people would not know the difference!

CHAPTER 87
A Walk Round A Stately Home

Just living is not enough...one must have sunshine, freedom and a little flower.
Hans Christian Andersen

The stately home that Harry's wedding was to be held in is owned by friends of the bride. We drove up to the Lakes the day before the wedding and decided to have a little peek at the venue. The house is in stunning parkland and surrounded by The Lakeland Fells. The long driveway is tree lined and as we turned on the gravel circle the lady of the house came out to speak to us.

When we introduced ourselves she was very accommodating and insisted on showing us round her home. The nineteenth century walled garden and the rose garden were spectacular and we enjoyed walking round in the sparkling May sunshine. We went inside the house to have afternoon tea of cucumber sandwiches and seed cake with a pot of Lapsong Souching tea.

THE LOTUS GENERATION

The oak, galleried landing and the sweeping staircase were breathtaking. The magnificent reception rooms were filled with the most amazing furniture and portraits. There were vases of fragrant lilies everywhere ready for the wedding next day. The smell of the flowers and the lavender polish on the centuries old furniture was intoxicating.

We went on our way feeling very happy and relaxed. This was to be my brother's third wedding and we were looking forward to it immensely. I was still friendly with his previous wives but thought Anne Marie was a perfect match for him in every way.

Grant had booked us in to a swish hostelry not far from where Harry and Anne-Marie's wedding was to be held. The satnav could not find the address and so Grant hit on the age old idea of going into the pub to ask directions. A kind old man came outside to point us in the right direction. A very narrow lane and a sharp left turn got us to the right house.

An attractive cream stone house was attached to some stables. As we got out of the car, the husband answered the door and greeted us with a fairly stern demeanour. I smiled, stepped over the doorstep and the first thing I noticed was that every available wall space was covered with pictures of him on a horse. He was sitting on a horse, jumping over a fence on a horse and standing next to a horse.

He insisted on revealing and describing every picture in minute detail as I swayed gently backwards and forwards. I had left hospital with lots of medication and had been warned to take things very easily. I had had a long day and I just wanted to lie down. The husband carried on talking and politeness dictated we maintain our frozen smiles.

There were photographs of him in America on a horse, in Dubai on a horse and in Paris on a horse and that was just one wall. At that point I actually swayed to the left violently and Grant caught me. We were eventually shown up to our room. It was cool and old fashioned with a four poster bed and dark furnishings but had a nice bathroom and dressing room.

I slept fitfully and the next morning we decided to go for a stroll on the beach. Of course we were away for far too long and we needed to rush to be ready on time for the wedding. I had brought three different outfits and matching hats to try out. A pink dress and jacket with a 1940s hat, a cream long dress and a floppy hat and a pale blue two piece suit with a fascinator. Every woman knows that feeling where you just cannot decide what to wear and so you fling things on and off, whilst getting hotter and hotter. Eventually with two minutes to go I looked in the mirror and thought "Yes, you look very appropriate for your brother's wedding" and we set off.

As I ran back in the bathroom to get my watch I glanced back around the room and realised that it was in a state of chaos .Hats, dresses, shoes, jewellery were strewn about. I actually said to Grant "Gosh this room is a bit dishevelled but nobody will be going inside it before we get back tonight"

As we rushed out the lady of the house was astride a very large horse on the driveway. We greeted her and Grant had to manoeuvre the car around her and consequently scraped his beautiful new blue jaguar on the dry stone wall. He smiled at her through gritted teeth.

CHAPTER 88
Meeting My Father's Partner

Marriage is an alliance entered into by a man can't sleep with the window shut and a woman who can't sleep with the window open.
George Bernard Shaw

The wedding was utterly delightful. My nieces Holly and Joanna were perfect bridesmaids in their mulberry coloured dresses and carried bouquets of cream roses and fragrant boughs of lavender. My nephews Edward and younger brother Rupert were so smart in their morning suits,

My new sister-in-law looked gorgeous and her dress drew a gasp from the assembled company. It was cream silk with a scoop neck and long ruched skirt. She looked as radiant as her teenage son Daniel who gave her away.

At the wedding breakfast Grant and I sat on a table with my father Murray and his new lady friend Stella. I had not met her before and did not know what to expect. It had been twenty years since my mother died and Murray had been single since then. I really warmed to her but found it a little disconcerting to see my father being affectionate towards a woman that was not my mother!

We were also sitting with my nephew Edward who is Harry's oldest son. We had never met his girlfriend Jessica before and I found her charming and intelligent. As we talked we realised that she had taught English at the school just around the corner from our house in Spain. Her parents were still in Spain and she met Ed the day after she came back here to teach Spanish in an English school.

The speeches were very funny and hit just the right note. Harry was still playing competitive rugby in his early fifties and all his team were there to support him. I had met them all at his fiftieth birthday party and danced to the music of Northern Soul era until my feet hurt.

Grant and I had been to a wedding recently where the father of the bride had fainted clean away as he started to speak. His wife was so embarrassed that she closed her eyes and taking her hat off laid her perfectly coiffured head on the table.

Just after the ceremony all the children ran outside to play as it was such a perfect early summer day. One of the bigger children hurried back in shouting that a cow had just given birth in the next field and all the children were in a circle watching.

A chap with ruddy cheeks who I took to be a farmer shouted very sternly "That is very, very dangerous" and the assembled company ran outside in their finery to see what was happening and who needed rescuing.

Order was restored and the dancing began and it was a chance for me to meet the newest babies in the family. I do not really know what happened but I was left in charge of several of them for some time. My favourite job!

Later on in the evening I danced with the groom and wished him much happiness. After a last waltz with my husband we said our goodbyes. It was not too sad however as the whole family was decamping to Greece in four days' time and so we would see them all very soon.

We drove back down the country lanes in companionable silence listening to Jamie Cullum on the radio. As Grant opened the door to our room I just wanted to sink on to the bed. As he put the lights on I really noticed the room and I felt my tiredness drain away. I could not believe my eyes.

I had definitely heard of the kitchen fairy but never in my life had I heard of the wedding outfit fairy. When I looked around I could see that every hat was back in its box, every piece of jewellery was rearranged, and my suitcase was packed beautifully with tissue paper between the layers. Even my underwear was folded neatly. I was in that peculiar distracting place between fury and shame. How dare they touch my things and why oh, why had I left the room in such disarray?

We went down to breakfast next morning and the wife passed me in the hall with her riding hat on her head and her crop in her hand. She stopped, smiled insouciantly and enquired whether we had a good stay in her establishment. I answered in the affirmative but said a little frostily "You know you really should have left my things for me to pack myself".

She threw her head back and a tinkling laugh escaped her lips and then she announced "Gosh darling, that was not me; Jeremy cannot bear anything out of place so he always tidies the guests' rooms"

We stayed for breakfast next day as Grant was starving. We chatted with a lovely couple and it turned out, as it very often does, that we had mutual friends in London. Grant paid the bill and he said goodbye.

As we left the white washed house I decided not to meet the gaze of the man who had rifled my drawers!

CHAPTER 89
We Are Off To Greece

There is the heat of love, the pulse of longing the lover's whisper, irresistible- magic to make the sanest man go mad.
Homer, the Iliad

We were only home forty-eight hours when we had to leave for the airport. I carefully packed my case for a week's holiday.

THE LOTUS GENERATION

In the interim I went for walk with my youngest granddaughter. It very often happens that a son's daughter takes after his mother and this was true in Ruby's case. She ran at life every day expecting an adventure and her wonderful laugh was so infectious.

This particular sunny June morning she was walking on the insurance company wall and I was holding her hand tightly. A pleasant young woman taking a morning stroll approached us with her twins in a pushchair. "Gosh, your daughter looks like you," she commented as she smiled.

"Thank you, she does, what gorgeous boys you have" I replied as we passed each other. It was a polite, nondescript exchange of greetings like millions of others every day all over the world.

She smiled back and suddenly a clear four year old voice piped up out of nowhere "Excuse me please, lady" the twins' mum looked back.

"I think you will find that I am actually her granddaughter and she is actually my grandmother, I think there is a possibility that she looks like me …. I do not really know." and then she tailed off.

Her words hung between us like so many deflating pink balloons falling slowly to earth. We were both struggling to contain our mirth.

The young American mum stared and we exchanged a conspiratorial smile and went on our merry way.

I had learned a packing lesson early on in life and always obeyed it. When a few of you are travelling together always split your clothes between cases. That way if someone's case is missing you always have clothes. I learned the lesson because my mother and father had been to Cuba many years before and his suitcase had gone missing. When father tried to buy clothes he learned that the average Cuban man's waist was thirty two inches and he was at thirty eight inch waist even when he breathed in his hardest. He spent three weeks in the same pair of trousers.

Whether it was vanity or the drugs I had taken in hospital I really just forgot the rule. I packed my case carefully, wedding clothes on one side, holiday clothes on the other. I packed my best pale blue fascinator on the top wrapped in tissue paper and included all the strong antibiotics I was still taking. There were eight different prescriptions in that new navy case.

We travelled to Greece with our daughter and her children. Miranda is much organised and she was determined to take care of her recently hospitalised mother. It was chilly in England so I travelled in my boots, jeans and leather jacket. Miranda did everything and we were met at Cephalonia airport by our son James who had already been out there a week with his family.

James helped us collect our suitcases as they arrived one by one. All of the suitcases that is, except for my new navy one with all my clothes and medication inside. We waited and waited and then reported it lost and then drove to the villa. When anybody asked me if I was upset I gave a cheery wave and said, "Oh its fine I will manage somehow."

Our room was in the basement of a gorgeous villa with an infinity pool and a glorious view. I sat on the bed in my jeans, boots and jacket. Greece was having a heat wave, it was 45 degrees outside. "Will you be Ok?," Grant asked solicitously. "I am going to be fine" I said graciously. "I have no shoes, no knickers, no clothes, nothing to wear for the wedding and most of all none of my important medication. How could I not be perfectly splendid?"

After lots of phone calls the next day it was established that my case was really missing. My beautiful clothes, my Majorcan pearls, my precious pale blue fascinator and most of all my urgent medication had gone into thin air. The most important thing now was that I really needed to find something to wear for the wedding. I also needed shoes for my size 8 feet. Then my daughter remembered that she had bought me a pair of pink Birkenstocks for my birthday and she had brought them in her case.

I went to the nearest shopping centre and discovered that the only clothes shop was a Chinese shop. I wandered about for hours trying to find something to wear. I eventually found a brown t-shirt made in Italy and a long orange skirt. The only other thing I managed to buy was a bright pink bra and a six pack of extra-large lime green knickers.

It turned out that one of my nieces had brought two wedding outfits with her because she could not decide between them. She kindly said that I could have the one she did not want to wear. I stood waiting whilst she looked at the outfits that she had laid out on her bed. One was a long loose fitting cream dress with a matching shawl and hat. The other was a short silver dress with a big belt and a low neck.

I hoped, well actually I prayed that she would choose the silver dress. Eventually she plumped for the long cream number leaving me with a shiny silver dress at least one size too small. It was a good job I did not try it on or else I would have run screaming from the room.

CHAPTER 90
A Wedding On The Beach

I shall wear white flannel trousers and walk along the beach.
T.S. Eliot

We settled in for the first night at the villa and had a delicious lamb kleftiko and honey laden baklava. We all went to bed early as the wedding was the next day.

The wedding ceremony was to be held on the beach near the villa in which we were staying. The rest of the hundred strong wedding party were in a luxury hotel on the other side of the town. I had not seen my sister Gillian who was the mother of the groom, for a few months and so I was looking forward to catching up with her.

The morning of the wedding arrived and we were all up bright and early. I put on my pink flip flops, lime green knickers, shocking pink bra and a size too small shiny silver dress. I put on my best smile but I refused to look in the mirror.

The posed question "Does my bum look big in this?" in the delightful 1998 novel by Arabella Weir, *Diary of an Insecure Woman* was condensed to one salient word in our house. As you patted your derriere you enquired of whoever was present "Callipygian?" [2] The answer was always a hilarious "No!"

I glanced around and as there was no one else in the room I left with my eyes closed and my hatless head held high.

---

[2] Having well shaped buttocks.

THE LOTUS GENERATION

The family looked lovely in all its colourful finery as we headed for the beach. The temperature was forty six degrees and more or less unbearable. There had really not been much point in putting on makeup as it slid off about two minutes later. Consequently we all had very pink faces with a pained expression on them as we walked along. My sister Gillian, the mother of the groom came towards me looking very elegant in black with her hair in a lovely chignon. Her feathered fascinator had an exquisite veil and black sequins. She looked perfect except for the ubiquitous pink face.

She had also made a gargantuan effort with mascara which was evident by the dark smudges around her watering eyes. Her first whispered words as she kissed me on both cheeks were "Help, it's so hot and I've got two pairs of Spanx on."

I just managed to give my two nephews, the groom Rufus and the best man Edward , a hug before we were required to be seated as the bride was about to arrive.

As I took my seat I had my first look at the surroundings and they took my breath away. The golden beach was lapped gently by the most perfect azure sea. We were sitting on white chairs that matched the flower strewn pergola under which they were about to be married. I closed my eyes and felt the sun on my face and the sound of water gently swishing first this way and then back again.

Rufus and Edward looked so handsome in their cream linen suits. They had been inseparable since they were small boys. They were cousins only three months apart in age and were still very much best friends.

I smiled deliciously to myself remembering the family Christmas shows that all the children used to put on for the grownups. Rufus and Edward always played their part but insisted on facing the wall when they were doing a rendition of a poem or a story as they were so shy. This went on until there were about twelve and I was so proud of the engineer and solicitor that they had become. I had a fleeting image of my mother Mona and wished she had been there to see this happy day.

CHAPTER 91
Your Bouquet Is Divine

Love is a friendship that has caught fire.
Anon.

The music started and the beautiful bride arrived on her beaming father's arm. Fiona looked exquisite in her fitted golden guipure lace dress. The bride and groom smiled lovingly at each other and the ceremony began. It was only then I noticed her beautifully handcrafted broach bouquet. The golden broaches, buttons and beads glinted in the sunshine. They were offset by turquoise and pale green stones. It was just glorious and perfect for the stiflingly hot day when fresh flowers would have wilted. Her delightful little blonde bridesmaid Isabella stood perfectly still smiling throughout and the cute little pageboy Fergus had his linen suit offset by a cowboy hat on top of his curls.

I was sitting next to my brother Harry and his new bride who were holding hands. They had only been married five days but had taken their honeymoon in Greece so they would not miss this wedding. I looked around and thought how lucky we were to have such a wonderful family.

After the ceremony finished I decided to head for the shade as I was still feeling very weak. I climbed up the five steps to the walkway and stopped to get my bearings.

Then I heard a voice I recognised behind me say "Would you give me a lift up please." Behind me on the beach was my little sister looking fabulous but in a skirt so tight she could not get up the steps. There is an unwritten law that when a little sister asks a big sister a favour she cannot refuse and so I bent down and put my shoulder under hers and heaved her up the steps. As we both stood breathless trying to speak in the stifling heat, my daughter, Miranda, ran towards us shouting, "Mother, what do you think you are doing, you have only just come out of hospital!"

She ushered us towards the shaded area with its cooling champagne on silver trays and welcome comfortable seats. We both thankfully collapsed with as much elegance as we could muster in the heat and each gave a little moan of pleasure. I just pushed my feet out of my pink flip flops but it took me several attempts to remove my sister's Kurt Geiger high heels. That was because every time I leant forward the world went round in a very alarming manner.

Slowly we all headed up to the restaurant where the reception was being held. It was in a very picturesque beachside setting with views of the mountains and orange groves. It was a white building reflecting the sun's rays but covered in the most delicious pink bougainvillea set off by pale green grapevines. At about 6pm the wedding breakfast began to arrive and it was still being served at midnight. The smiling waiters and waitresses just kept gliding around the tables with large silver platters of food and bottles of ice cold white wine.

First to be served to the table came the meze dishes, spanakopita (spinach and cheese pies), dolmades (stuffed vines leaves), and keftedes (Greek meatballs). The next course was a selection of peppers, cucumber and carrots with hummus and tzatziki dips.

As the music started the main course arrived. There was a choice of lamb kleftico, beef stifado and spit roast baby lamb. There was also a plentiful supply of fresh fish including squid, prawns the local white fish cooked with garlic and tomatoes the vegetables were fabulous Greek salad with olives and feta cheese and herb crusted potatoes.

After most guests had eaten their main course the traditional Greek dancing display started. The women's costumes were demure with their blue almost floor length skirts, elegantly stitched in a flowing light material. They wore matching jackets with white frills around their wrists. The men looked more severe in maroon trousers and jackets. Their traditional garb stood out the most though; the white pleated skirts called the Phoustanella were reminiscent of every Greek picture I had ever seen.

Greek dancing or Horos is a very old tradition referred to as far back as in Plato's time. Traditional dancing takes place at times of celebration such as weddings, Easter or the grape harvest. Each area has its own style of dance and there is always a strict hierarchy in which the dancers perform. The speed of the dance was so frenetic that the audience had to stand back for fear of being caught by a swirling arm or a rogue pointed swinging foot.

CHAPTER 92
We Toast With Ouzo Over Here

You don't develop courage by being happy in your relationship everyday. You develop it by surviving difficult times and challenging adversity.

Epicuras

As dusk turned into a midnight sky the sparkling lights dotted here and there gave the most magical glow and all around you could see babies and toddlers dozing off on their parents laps or snuggling down in pushchairs everywhere.

The speeches came next with ouzo to toast the health of the bride and groom. They had lots of friends from school and university days as well as family from as far afield as Texas. Then the desert courses arrived with sweetmeats, honey coated baklava, strawberry cheesecake and fruit of every different variety as well as the gorgeous chocolate wedding cake.

I found myself leaning on the restaurant garden fence looking out to sea through the green and white swathe, watching a glorious rose coloured sunset. The noise of the wedding was far behind me. In front of me firmly ensconced in my grasp was my three year old grandson, Hugo. "How are we going to get home from this place, Granny?," was his question. "We will fly on a plane, darling" was my answer.

As I put my face against his warm blonde head he asked "Granny, why do you love me more than you love my Daddy, when he is your son?" I thought for a moment then I said "Well I love you both the same darling, it's just that I get to spend a lot of time with you when your Daddy is at work."

There was a moment's quiet and then he said "Is it Ok if I love my Mummy and Daddy just a little bit more than I love you?"

"Of course it is, darling, that is the way it is meant to be and don't forget that love is like an elastic band, it's always stretching to let new people in."

He breathed deeply as I had answered in the affirmative and content he wriggled down to join the dancing.

As I raced to keep up with him I pondered on the amazing things that go through a small child's mind. As I caught up with him and swooped him up, I handed him to my granddaughter, Ellie, who was now a beautiful and capable ten year old. I had spent two years looking after her for three days a week when she was small and my daughter resumed her career. I think they were the happiest days of my life. Small children's minds are wondrous things.

I joined in the frenetic dancing and was swung around by my darling eight year old Felix and almost lost my balance in my flip flops.

Thankfully as coffee was served the Greek dancers came back out and soon the assembled company was up dancing, slapping their heels and whirling around. Suddenly the waiters were out again with Moussaka and salad for the assembled company and everybody had decided they were hungry again.

I was just looking round at so many people having such a good time when I realised my daughter-in-law Emma was ready to go back to the villa. She was seven and a half months pregnant with my newest grandson and so I had arranged to share a taxi with her and her children back home.

When we got back to the villa I finally decided to look in the mirror. I could not believe my eyes. I looked like a shiny silver paper clad astronaut strangled tightly in the middle by string. The Chinese bright pink bra had given me a cleavage that I did not normally possess but at least the colour matched my flip flops. I really hoped nobody had taken a photo of me as I really was not going to live this down in a hurry.

I finally fell asleep and was awakened by my husband climbing into bed. He whispered, "Everyone is back except Miranda and James and they were both too busy dancing to think about coming home yet." No matter how old your children are you worry and that is just a fact of life.

I swung my legs out of bed onto the tiles which were still warm with the residual heat of the day. I looked around for clothes and pulled the long orange Chinese skirt up under my arms so it looked like a dress. I walked into the kitchen to get a glass of water and so began my poolside vigil.

The hours ticked slowly by and the sun was just peeping out of its hiding place into the pearly pink horizon. The swifts had just begun their early morning diving party at the pool and they did not care a fig for me as I sat and watched their acrobatics. I heard my children, before I spied them, chatting away and laughing together. The early dawn was still misty as they came over the brow of the hill arm in arm after having walked the considerable distance from the wedding reception.

I returned the favour a few nights later when we went to spend a few hours with my brother Harry at his hotel. We left later than we intended and took the wrong route home. We were in a very rural area and our phones did not work. It was about two am when we finally arrived up the hill. As we walked around the corner of the villa we were met by the steely gaze of our children who had been very concerned.

After telling us they had been very concerned for our welfare they went to bed but we stayed up for a while enjoying the moonlight reflecting in the infinity pool and the sound of crickets chirping away the night. I put my feet up on the chair with a little squeak as lizards slithered around the warm terrace.

Grant went back into the kitchen and came back out with fat purple olives, salty feta and soft squishy baklava dripping with sweet honey. He came back out with the tray garnished with a sprig of oleander that was growing by the kitchen door. "Ah" I thought "so romance is not dead in this corner of Hellenic paradise."

CHAPTER 93
Melons In Mirabelle?

Skiing is a dance and the mountain always leads.
Anon.

Miranda and James had always been best buddies from childhood but family and work commitments meant they did not spend as much time together now. However they always holidayed together with their families every summer and Grant and I were always invited along as well.

The last trip had been a skiing trip to Mirabelle in France. I am not much of a skier but I do enjoy an alpine view and a steaming mug of hot chocolate whilst looking after little people, too young to go in a ski lift. The sight of your family coming one by one over the hill in their multi coloured finery on their skis is just delightful. I love the après ski, the shopping, the afternoon cake that the chalet maid makes and all things to do with skiing. Just please don't ask me to fling myself down a mountain on a very narrow shiny locomotive.

Grant and I always get up early in a morning when we are on holiday to savour those lovely early morning hours with the grandchildren. We especially loved going on the early morning shopping run and letting the children choose whatever they want, much to the parents chagrin. My stock answer has always been "You can have it of course….. It's the holiday".

I had been hoisted with my own petard the year before when I had holidayed with my daughter and her two children aged eight and ten. We were in Mirabelle and I had taken the children to the tiny supermarket on the top of the hill... As usual we had all picked what we wanted as we were on holiday. Our basket of goods included, melons, avocados chocolate, peaches, pomegranate, yoghurt and strawberries. My eyes watered as the till finished pinging. My daughter laughed her head off saying "Oh Mother, only you could buy avocadoes and strawberries up a mountain!"

This particular bright, sunny Greek morning we were not going shopping we were off to see the loggerhead turtles. We had been told that they were the only turtles that nested in Greece. The logger head turtle is different because it is a reddish brown colour and has a big head. The turtles in Kefalonis include about 80 females on Mouda which is their main nesting beach.

We were lucky because to the children's delight we were able to see them. The older children were interested in the story of the turtles. Large turtles can weigh over 100 kilos and become a meter in length. They lay four nests a season with 100 eggs in each nest. The nesting season lasts from June until August and the baby turtles hatch about 8 weeks after being laid in chambers about 30 metres from the water's edge.

We arrived home to be given great credit for an educational trip and the children spent the morning playing with their turtle toys and writing on their turtle notepaper with their turtle pens.

CHAPTER 94
Our Annual Birthday Bash

A granddaughter completes the unbroken circle of love.
Anon.

That evening we went back to the wedding breakfast restaurant for another night of Greek dancing and feasting. This was a little more relaxed and in my opinion the dancing was on the dangerous side. I spent the evening looking after small children to keep them safe from wildly, whirling untrained dancer's feet.

It was only at midnight as the birthday cake was brought out that I remembered it was our birthday. My granddaughter Ellie and I have birthdays one day apart and since she has been old enough we have a joint celebration at midnight. The singing and celebrations had just started in earnest but to be honest I was so tired from being chief child minder that day that I fell fast asleep in a comfortable beach chair.

The next day I rang my sister Gillian and suggested we had a trip out with her and her husband. The four of us had been good friends from school days. Grant and I drove the thirty minute journey across to their hotel. The only hire car we could get was a Fiat and there a lot of huffing and puffing as we all tried to get inside the car.

Eventually we set off with the idea of seeing some sights and then having a late lunch. We were all so hot and squashed that the idea of a restaurant by the water seemed very seductive and so we stopped at the next likely looking place.

Lots of the wedding guests were there as well so we waved a cheery hello and were escorted to our table. The patron in his starched white apron was shouting in Greek to all his staff to hurry and scurry. They rushed around with Greek salads, kleftico, mousaka and aubergines of every hue. There was also lots of ice cream because there were many children in the extended party.

Eventually Gillian, Malcolm, Grant and I were the only people left in the restaurant as the afternoon light mellowed into a perfect dusk. As Grant was the designated driver the other three of us were actually quite mellow on the wine and liqueurs that were being offered.

THE LOTUS GENERATION

The tanned, handsome, middle aged owner of the restaurant came out and smiled at us and nodded towards the beautiful view. We all smiled and looked at each other. As the liqueur had loosened my tongue a little I decided to discuss the state of the Greek economy with him. "That was a delicious meal thank you, but are you finding that you are less busy this year with the dip in the economy?"

The Greek restaurant owner put his head on one side, and peered out at the sea for long time. I vaguely wondered if he hadn't understood me. "Actually love, I live near Blackpool and I am only out here for a few months because my elderly father is ill," he replied with a broad Lancashire accent. "The kids are all bored with the sunshine and want to get back to their lives".

As we chatted with this kind, hospitable man I could hear the sounds of *Rolling in the Deep* by Adele being played somewhere behind me and I thought "We are slowly all becoming Europeans."

After he had taken his apron off and joined us as the table, he waved the waiter over with more drinks and after much discussion it turned out he lived round the corner from my sister-in-law!

CHAPTER 95
A Long Slow Breath

Life is what you make it. Always has been always will be.
Grandma Moses

The next morning I was awake early and decided to go for a walk on my own. I left a note on my pillow and climbed up the steps and on to the gravel road. I had a small map that I had been given in the supermarket and looked around to find the direct route to the sea.

I love company and have always enjoyed being around people. However I now understood the value of being alone with my own thoughts. About five years ago during a particularly busy work and personal time I had finally asked myself a question, "Where can I find some calm in my ever more chaotic world?"

I began to research this question. One of my answers came in the form of mindfulness or being present in the moment. In my experience, that means bringing my complete attention to the present moment.

Before I begin I start to focus my attention on calming my breathing. Calm breathing involves taking smooth, slow regular breaths.

I take a slow breath in through the nose, breathing into my lower tummy for about four seconds. (I lay my hand on my tummy to remind myself.)

I hold my breath for two seconds. Then I exhale slowly through my mouth for about four seconds. I then wait two or three seconds before taking another breath.

It is so hard not to worry about the future or dwell on past mistakes. We cannot help it as it is the human condition. However if you can put everything out of your mind except for the one thing that you are now experiencing then you will be totally at ease.

Mindfulness means focusing on the taste of the ice cream you are eating, the scent of bunch of roses on your desk, the sight of the pink and orange sunset in the distance or the look on your lover's face. To be in the moment, you need to bring your senses alive.

We all have five senses sight, touch, sound, taste and smell. Make time to really focus on them all one by one.

Stop and think. What can you see now? The myriad array of colours shapes and sizes around you and the shades of light of light and dark. Is what you are concentrating near you or far away? Are you in the picture or looking at from the outside?

Then close your eyes if it is safe to do so and really focus on your hearing. Is that laughter you can hear in the distance, the perfect bird song, the wind rustling in the trees?

Now can you feel anything? Your bare feet on the grass, the soft chair under your legs, the wind in your hair or the sun on your face?

Then last of all focus on what you can smell and taste, the perfume of the roses or the delicious taste of the pumpkin soup.

Once your breathing is calm and your attention is focused let yourself really enjoy this perfect experience.

CHAPTER 96
Gosh! I Thought You Were Still In The Shower

Fish to taste right must swim three times, in water, in butter and in wine.
Polish proverb

I began to walk along the path and took a deep breath. It was a lovely bright summer's morning. There was not a cloud in the azure sky and the pink sunrise cast a pearlescent glow over everything it caressed. I closed my eyes for a moment and reached blindly for the scent in the air.

Whatever it was, it whisked me away to my kitchen and towards the vats of tomato sauce I was prone to make on a weekend without a plan. Then I recognised the wild oregano and thyme that were growing all around me. As I was stepping on them the scented oils were being released into the air around me.

As I stood looking down, the faintest of breezes made a serene, whispering sound as it travelled across the top of the long grass. I looked down the hill and noticed a narrow winding path that I had missed as I rushed past in the car. I looked around and decided to follow the trammelled pathway; I had my phone with me so I felt a burgeoning confidence.

I could see a lemon grove in the distance and decided to head for that. The sun was out now and I could feel its gentle warmth on my head. I took a deep breath and relaxed my shoulders. The scent of the lemons reached me first, sharp and pungent and utterly intoxicating.

Beyond the grove I could see the sea. The blue water was sparkling and shimmering with millions of diamond shapes. As I focused my attention on the lemons I could see that some of them were as big as a tennis ball. I leant forward and placed my warm face in amongst the light green leaves and breathed in the lemony air. I had never felt more alive.

My feet began to move easily down the path and I felt full in control of my downward journey. It was then I noticed the plume of colours amongst the green of the wild herbs and grasses. There were blue cornflowers to match the sea, startling red poppies and many varieties of pure white flowers that I did not recognise.

THE LOTUS GENERATION

Suddenly as I rounded a corner I juddered to a halt as I realised my feet were now lovely and warm. The path had finished and through my sandals I could sense the perfect white sand. I bent down to remove them and scooped up a handful of sand. I allowed the sharp, tiny grains to trickle through my fingers. I noticed with surprise that my finger nails were painted the same colour as the pink sunrise. I walked over to the shore and slowly followed the water's edge allowing the cool water to lap against my free toes.

I stood for a moment and drank in the life energy that was all around me.

A delicious smell of coffee invaded my thoughts and I began to look up. There was a small beach café in the near distance. I quickened my step and soon arrived at the source of the coffee aroma. There were a few locals enjoying the early morning.

I recognised the lady at the counter as she waved at me. She ran the bakery in the village nearest to our villa. She picked up her order of olives and paté and signalled to ask if I wanted a lift with her back to the villa. I grabbed my coffee to go with a big smile of thanks.

I perched on the side of her bread delivery van and we began the tortuous, perpendicular climb. I began to feel a nibble of anxiety at the corner of my brain but firmly dismissed it. I climbed out, with wobbly knees, from the van and waved a cheery farewell to my companion. My adventure ended as I rounded the corner with an armful of fresh bread for our party. They were all around the table on the terrace and were cheered by the smell of the new bread to go with their breakfast.

My husband stared at me quizzically as he pulled out a chair for me, "I did not even realise you had gone out, I really thought that you were still in the shower."

CHAPTER 97
Two Brides In The Shade

A man is incomplete until he is married. Then he is finished!
Zsa Zsa Gabor

A couple of days later we rose late and decided to go out for a lunch. It was about four pm when our caravan of three hire cars stopped to look at the map. A young Greek woman outside an empty vine covered taverna shouted across to us. "Hi there, I have plenty of shade in here and I will promise I will cook you whatever you want to eat today"

The offer was too tempting as we were all so hot and so we trooped in a file into a lovely space that as promised, was cool and airy.

There were dahlias stuffed in antique jugs all placed around the room. She brought us similar jugs of iced homemade lemonade which the children loved and white wine which the adults thought delicious.

I looked up and down the assembled company and realised with delight that both the honeymoon couples were here with us. They had each been out driving and seen our cars outside the restaurant and decided to stop and join us for lunch.

I smiled at our host as she came back into dining room and she beckoned me to follow her into the kitchen. It was decorated with cool white tiles decorated with bunches of grapes and vine leaves. There were baskets of courgettes with their flowers still attached and shiny deep purple aubergines sitting up proud in baskets on the counter.

She opened the kitchen door to show me her garden stuffed full of herbs and I noticed red tomatoes as big as your fist that were warming themselves in the afternoon sun. The fragrant smell of bushes of Greek basil and the fat ripe tomatoes was intoxicating. I also noticed the rows of brightly coloured dahlias that she grew herself.

Her husband appeared around the corner with his starched white apron on and opened a large chest freezer with every kind of homemade traditional Greek dish stuffed inside. Then he showed me the fridge which was bursting with soft cheeses, purple olives and glistening pink prawns.

CHAPTER 98
The Whole Family Is Together Again

Gossip is the act of saying nothing in a way that leaves practically nothing unsaid.

Walter Winchell

I stepped down the steep marble steps and went through the plastic iridescent beaded door curtain that separated the private and public areas. I looked around the restaurant and counted that there were twenty-four of us including six children in our party.

Lunch today was my treat and so I went bag up the steps and said, "Lets agree on a fair amount now for everything and then you can bring us the best of your Greek dishes for us all to share. The only thing I ask is that you feed the children straight away and you bring the rest of us some meze as soon as you can, please. "

Shimmering white china bowls of Greek salad and matching plates of feta cheese sprinkled with honey and dried oregano suddenly appeared from the kitchen. Then suddenly the sweet smelling delicious fresh bread filled the table as soon as I sat down and rustic dishes of hummus, taramaslata and tzatziki quickly followed.

So began one of the best afternoons I ever had in all of my life. The joyful Greek music played along in the background as we ate and talked long into the afternoon and early evening. Crispy courgette flowers with a cheese and pine nut filling, roasted, striped baby aubergines, and enough crispy squid for everyone to have their fill was just the start. The bottles of delicious, white wine flowed around the table giving the poor designated drivers a wide berth. We rounded it all off with the biggest, sweetest baklava I had ever seen and tiny cups of delicious coffee.

Whilst we had been chatting to the taverna owner she suddenly realised that we had two brides in our midst. She ran back out of the kitchen door and as we left her Taverna with much formality as she presented both brides with a bouquet of sweet smelling roses from her kitchen garden and wished us well. Hospitality indeed!

THE LOTUS GENERATION

A perfect time was had by all that week. We spent a wonderful time with our children and grandchildren swimming and playing on the beach. We also spent a lot of time with our siblings and their children and grandchildren which was an exquisite treat for the whole family.

As I watched all the children running in and out of the sea I could hear the family laughing and chatting and I thought it was such a shame that our mother had not lived to see this heart-warming sight.

I cheered myself with the thought that she would be watching from wherever she was.

CHAPTER 99
Home Again, Home Again

Life loves to be taken by the lapel and told, "I am with you kid. Let's go!"

Maya Angelou

When we arrived back in England I was still wearing one of my fetching orange Chinese shop outfits and a straw hat bedecked with flowers. My always smartly dressed alter ego had learned a powerful and humbling lesson that week.

I was still in that glorious state of holiday euphoria. Suddenly I heard my name mentioned and I was instructed over the airport tannoy to present myself to the customer service desk.

I trundled across to the designated area and a straight-faced young woman smiled a wan smile that did not quite reach her eyes and carefully checked my just about to run out passport.

She spent some time checking me up and down, quite rudely I thought. Did this older, blonde, orange bedecked, tanned creature in white pumps match the serious brunette of ten years ago?

She sighed, a highly professional sigh and then finally she inclined her perfectly coiffured head towards the corner of her office.

There waiting in all its beaten up glory was my recalcitrant case. The airport lady studiously read and then re-read the paperwork and then said it transpired that my poor suitcase had actually been on a convoluted world trip.

It had had its locks blown open by the authorities and was covered in finger prints and various customs sticky labels and tied with string. As I tentatively opened my still new but very definitely now shabby, chic navy case I could see my Majorcan pearls, my precious blue fascinator and enough boxes of heavy duty antibiotics to ward off every bug known to man for a very, very long time.

***

AFTERWORD

The Lotus Generation[3]

Those people between the ages of 55 and 75 plus, who have grasped the freedom to experience a different type of life and go gallivanting*.

SOME USEFUL NLP PRESUPOSITIONS

1 Communication is more than what you are saying.
2 No-one is wrong or broken. People work perfectly to accomplish what they are accomplishing.
3 People already have all the resources they need.
4 Behind every human behaviour is a positive intention.
5 All behaviour is useful is some context.
6 The meaning of communication is the response that you get.
7 If you are not getting the response you want, try something different.
8 There is no such thing as failure only feedback.
9 Having choice is better than having no choice at all.
10. In any system the element with the most flexibility exerts the most influence.
11 The map is not the territory.
12 If someone can do something anyone can do it.
13 You cannot fail to communicate.

---

[3] To visit or go to a lot of different places, enjoying themselves and not worry too much about the other things they "should" be doing!

Recipes from our Travels

1 French Bakers Gateaux Noir Recipe

125g Flour
170g Unsalted butter
200g Ground walnuts
200g Sugar
4 eggs
100g bitter chocolate
1tsp baking powder
12 walnut halves

    Mix the flour and most of the butter until crumbly. Stir in the nuts, baking powder and half the sugar. Stir in the beaten egg yolks. Whisk the egg whites with the sugar and fold meringue in to nut mixture.

    Place in an eight inch baking tin then bake for 20 minute in a medium oven. Then melt chocolate with a little of the reserved butter and pour onto the cake to glaze. Decorate with walnut halves. It is perfectly delicious for afternoon tea with Earl Grey in a china cup.

2 Aunt Jane's Nanaimo Bars

Nanaimo Bars are three layer biscuits.
Ingredients
The base layer
112 grams butter
50 grams sugar
30 grams cocoa
a little milk
I beaten egg
1tsp of vanilla
30 grams each of shredded coconut and chopped walnuts
 200 grams of digestive biscuits/graham crackers
Middle layer
80 grams butter
6 tablespoons of milk
4 tbsps. Of custard powder

Icing sugar to taste
Top layer
8 oz. chocolate
1 tbsp. of butter. To cook Mix together the first 6 ingredients together over medium heat and then add coconut, walnuts and digestives. Pack into greased baking tin. Beat middle layer ingredients and pour over base. Warm chocolate and butter then pore over and leave to cool. Cut into squares and enjoy with a cup of coffee.

3 Aunt Amy's Quick chowder

4 potatoes
one large onion, and bunch of spring onions
1 can evaporated milk
1 small carton double cream
4oz butter
6 oz. bacon chopped
1 tin of corn
3 tins of clams

Fry chopped onion and bacon then add cubed potatoes and enough water to cover. Cook until potatoes are soft. Add the clams and juice and then add evaporated milk, cream and butter. Stir and warm through but do not boil. Serve in a crusty loaf with crispy bacon and cracker topping.

4 My Recipe for Crema Catalana

This desert is easy to make and popular for the Spanish equivalent of Father's Day, St Joseph's Day

Ingredients
1 cup white sugar
4 egg yolks
2 cups of milk
1 cup of double cream
1 tablespoon of corn flour
1 teaspoon of lemon zest
2 tablespoons of caster sugar (to caramelise the top.)

Beat together sugar and egg yolks until it turns pale and frothy and then add lemon zest. Pour in milk and cream mixed with cornflour and mix well. Put the pan on a medium light and just stand and stir until you feel the mixture thicken. Ladle into small oven-proof dishes and put into the fridge to go cold. At least four hours. Sprinkle the sugar equally between dishes and put under a pre-heated grill until they caramelise. This may take between five and ten minutes so watch carefully. Put the Crema Catalana in the fridge until the caramel topping sets so you can crack it with a spoon. Delicious and moreish

5 Grant's favourite fish soup
1 kilo of white fish filleted
5 cups of water
Juice of 2 lemons and 4 oranges
1 red onion,
4 cloves of garlic
1 large ripe tomato
Pinch saffron, salt pepper, paprika to taste
5 small potatoes
Olive oil and parsley

Bring a large pan of water to the boil and add fish trimmings and orange peel, salt and pepper. Simmer for twenty minutes to make stock. Heat the oil, fry onions and garlic before adding fish stock to pan.

Cut potatoes in half and simmer in stock until soft. When potatoes are ready place the fish fillets cut into bite size pieces add and then simmer being careful not to let it boil. After 12 minutes then add the paprika, chopped tomato, orange and lemon juice and serve soup with parsley sprinkled on top. I serve this dish with Aioli (Spanish Garlic Mayonnaise) and crusty bread.

6 My Recipe for Spanakopita
10 sheets of filo pastry
250 g of feta cheese
150 full fat ricotta
25g parmesan
Bunch of spring onions
3 garlic cloves

1 red onion
Kilo spinach
1 tbs chopped dill
grated nutmeg
4 eggs
120g melted butter
1/4 cup olive oil
180 degree oven

Fry chopped onions and garlic until soft, add spinach and cook until soft. Cool pan then stir in cheeses, eggs, nutmeg, salt and pepper.

Butter oven proof 21/2 litre dish, lay in sheet of filo, brush with melted butter and repeat five times. Add cheese mixture and then lay another buttered sheet of filo, five times. Trim excess pastry, butter and score diamonds in top.

Bake for 45 minutes until golden brown, sprinkle more butter and dill on top. Serve warm with salad

7 The Unicorn Lady's Pulled Pork Recipe
(This cooks best in the slow cooker)

3 llbs of shoulder of pork

3 ozs dark brown sugar

I teaspoon each of chilli powder, cumin, cinnamon, salt & paprika

3 cloves of garlic and 4 red onions chopped and fried in olive Oil then covered with chicken stock

Pineapple juice to taste

Rub the sugar and spice mix into pork and then place on top of fried onions, garlic and stock in slow cooker.

Pour over pineapple juice.

Leave for about six hours on auto and then shred the juicy pork. Serve in bread rolls with your favourite barbeque sauce a side of coleslaw.

**